T0188796

Fight Fire with Fire

Proactive Cybersecurity Strategies for Today's Leaders

RENEE TARUN

Deputy CISO, Fortinet

WILEY

To my family, Brett, Ryan, and Rebecca,
for their continuous support and inspiration.

—Renee Tarun, Deputy CISO, Fortinet

About the Author

R ENEE TARUN IS THE DEPUTY CISO AT Fortinet. She has over twenty-five years of experience in information technology and cyber within the US Intelligence Community, Department of Defense, and law enforcement as well as private-sector entities around the world.

Renee has focused on enterprise security, compliance and governance, and product security at Fortinet. Prior to joining Fortinet, she served as Special Assistant to the Director of the National Security Agency (NSA) for Cyber and as Director of NSA's Cyber Task Force, where she shaped agency strategy as well as national cyber policy for the White House.

In addition, Renee served in many other roles concentrating on development and engineering, cyber strategy, operations, resourcing, and relationship management for the NSA, the Department of Defense, and the US Secret Service.

Renee is a board member for the George Mason University Volgenau School of Engineering and is co-author of *Cyber Safe*, a book aimed at keeping children safe online.

Acknowledgments

THIS BOOK HAS BEEN A COLLABORATIVE TEAM EFFORT involving many diverse cyber leaders and experts from across government and the private sector. It would not have been possible without their insightful contributions and thought leadership. Their dedication and energy continue to push boundaries and make our cyber world safer and more secure.

I would like to thank the entire Fortinet team for supporting me in the creation of this book, and for providing me with the opportunity to share insight and knowledge that will help guide technology leaders around the world.

Contributors

Sonia E. Arista

Marianne Bailey

Fatima Boolani

Beth-Anne Bygum

Laura Deaner

Lisa Donnan

Suzanne Hartin

Susan Koski

Jenny Menna

Mel T. Migriño

Sanju Misra

Terry Roberts

Maria S. Thompson

Anne Marie Zettlemoyer

Contents

Introduction

RENEE TARUN

D IGITAL TRANSFORMATION AND THE EVER-CHANGING THREAT landscape have significantly altered the role of chief information security officers (CISOs) and security decision-makers.

Traditional CISO responsibilities such as patch management and incident response are as critical as ever, but today's CISOs must also concern themselves with supply chain risks, myriad privacy regulations, and 5G. In addition to fighting traditional and emerging threats, CISOs also face the stress of the skills gap: not having enough people to do the job.

These challenges interwoven with network security are forcing CISOs to take a more holistic approach to balancing risk, security, and strategic business enablement.

Technology is not the only approach to solving the quagmire of security challenges we face. Security leaders must address people, processes, and technology, synthesizing them to create security solutions that manage risk while advancing business objectives at the speed of today's economy.

As CISOs, we must become fluent in the language of the business. We must influence others to change their mindsets, habits, and approaches to technology and behave in ways that maintain security. We need a cultural shift that enables everyone to adopt effective, ongoing processes to keep our organizations safe. Security must be embedded into vendor selection, employee onboarding, and product development. Security awareness training must be continuous to match the cadence of the threats we face.

We need security leaders who understand the value of the latest technology, but even more importantly who have the skills to develop relationships that bring people together and the discipline to create repeatable processes.

How Can We Be Effective CISOs?

Today's security leaders face considerable stress. The CISO role has a high turnover rate, with an average tenure of just twenty-six months. Fundamental changes are needed to empower us to lead effectively, attain a better work-life balance, and manage the inevitable stress of our roles. The answer is not working longer hours; 95% of CISOs are working an average of ten hours more a week than their contracts stipulate.[1]

We need shortcuts to success, like learning from mentors and peers. The challenge, of course, is finding the time for that learning. That's why my colleagues and I wrote this book: to share our knowledge and, more importantly, our experience, something that you will not find in a textbook or on a certification exam. We have come together to share our perspectives as security leaders from across industries and sectors, offering our best thinking as well as sharing important lessons learned. Harnessing this insight and utilizing the strategies in this book can help leaders and organizations improve their culture and security posture.

Who This Book Is For

With the ongoing evolution in security challenges and the pressing need for a cultural shift, this book identifies steps that we as leaders need to be thinking about. This book is for anyone working in cybersecurity and IT leadership who seeks a better grasp of the continually changing nature of security threats and who is interested in effective approaches to address them.

We also hope this book will inspire a more diverse group of people to consider a career in cybersecurity leadership. As we discuss in Chapter 5, there are both a skills gap and a diversity gap to fill in the world of cybersecurity.

By the time you finish this book, you will be evolving into a next-generation CISO. You will better understand how to adopt best practices and processes to encourage your people to make effective, safe use of technology. You will know how to serve as a business strategist, helping your organization reframe security as a business enabler. You will also learn how to improve security 24/7, up and down your supply chain, from the edge to the cloud, and from frontline workers up to your board. Finally, you will gain strategies to attract and promote the next generation of diverse talent.

Let's get started.

Note

1. https://nominetcyber.com/nominet-ciso-stress-report-one-year-on/

PART ONE
People

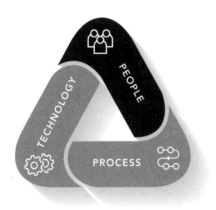

CYBERSECURITY IS NO LONGER ONLY THE DOMAIN OF I.T. AND security teams. From the loading dock to the C-suite, everyone must be security minded.

Within your organization, a well-trained staff can be your best line of cyber defense. But people can also be your worst enemies. You can buy top-of-the-line security technology and implement best practices, but if your people won't follow good security practices and policies or use that technology properly, your organization remains at risk. You must also get buy-in from your board of directors to create a culture of security.

How the CISO Role Is Evolving

What's the most important skill set for being a CISO? Current knowledge of the latest threats? Deep understanding of cybersecurity technology to mitigate security risks? Familiarity with the latest tools, tactics, procedures, and activities of well-funded hacking collectives?

Tech knowledge is not the most important characteristic of a CISO today.

Increasingly, CISOs are being elevated to the C-suite and becoming trusted business advisors. This requires soft skills, with the ability to communicate in terms that everyone understands. The CISO must be a business enabler and a strategic advisor who explains risk in business terms. Chapter 1 discusses the evolution of this critical role so you can focus your efforts on becoming a strong security leader.

Getting the Board on Board

Corporate boards are becoming more focused on cybersecurity than they have been in the past. Board members are beginning to understand that a security threat is not just a problem for the security team but a risk to the entire business.

Inadequate cybersecurity can expose employee and client data and put your organization at risk of failing to comply with privacy regulations. Weak security can also expose proprietary business information. In factories, weak cybersecurity can lead to injuries and even deaths. Poor cybersecurity can lead to lost revenue, lost reputation, lawsuits, and fines. When a breach happens in an organization, the fallout impacts revenue, operations, shareholders, and the entire business.

Increasingly, CISOs are requested to brief board members and answer questions regarding cybersecurity. If CISOs are fortunate, cybersecurity even helps drive board-level business decisions.

When speaking to the board, CISOs must learn to transition from tech talk to business strategy and risk and from troubleshooting tactical problems to looking at the big picture. Your team has to give board members the information they need to make decisions about cybersecurity and drive company direction, framed in a business context. So what should you know about speaking to the board? Chapter 2 covers this important topic.

Building a Culture of Security

Security is not a separate aspect of your business. As we'll see, security must be thought of and included in every process. Humans can often be the weakest link in cyber defenses. They usually want to do the right thing, but they need to fully understand their responsibilities with regard to cybersecurity.

A comprehensive all-in approach to security is needed across the business to drive security into your organizational DNA. It starts with the board but should also incorporate key ambassadors across business units to create a culture of security. These ambassadors bring specificity to the culture as it applies to each business area, offering examples for following good practices and policies.

Although security is a serious issue, security training doesn't have to be. Look to utilize initiatives that are fun and interactive to engage the workforce: think gamification. Rather than an annual approach to security training, awareness should be continuous throughout the year.

As more people work remotely, the need is growing for cybersecurity training that addresses multiple work environments. Employees need security awareness training to address a number of potential issues that arise both in traditional office environments as well as in home offices.

Building a strong security culture has a lasting impact on your organization. But your security culture must not stop with your internal processes; it should permeate your dealings with customers and business partners. It should be built into the products, services, and solutions that you provide to others.

How can you promote a culture where cybersecurity becomes everyone's responsibility? Chapter 3 offers strategies for building a culture of security, a culture that will be strengthened by processes in Part II and technology in Part III.

Mitigating Today's Threats

Today's threats have greatly evolved, and the nature of the adversary has evolved as well. Lone hackers, hackers for hire, and small collectives still exist, their numbers growing as online materials enable almost anyone to become a hacker. Exploits are bought and sold as a commodity on the dark web and are readily available to any of these adversaries. Today, however, these attackers are joined by well-funded adversaries from organized crime rings around the world as well as government-supported hacking groups from particular nation-states.

Your security posture must be strong enough to prevent a wide variety of outsiders from gaining access to your private and proprietary data, your processes, and your machines.

Unfortunately not all of your malicious adversaries are outside your enterprise. Sadly, some threat actors have inside access to your systems, including disgruntled or unethical current and former employees misusing access and data for personal gain or simply to cause trouble. Other potential insider threats include suppliers, partners, board members, and anyone else who has access to your systems and data.

There are other internal threats. We call them accidental insiders. You might call them humans. Accidental insiders expose the organization unintentionally because they are untrained, overworked, or unmotivated. These folks become threats when they respond to phishing attempts, use weak or default passwords, share passwords, leave devices unpatched or unlocked, and work over unsecured Wi-Fi networks.

Your organization is up against well-funded adversaries as well as people who might just press the wrong key. You'll learn about the many players behind today's evolving threats in Chapter 4.

Addressing the Skills and Diversity Gaps

The gap between the number of cybersecurity workers we have and the number we need is widening. As of 2021, more than 3 million cybersecurity workers are needed globally, according to the (ISC)² Cybersecurity Workforce Study.[1] More than 65% of all organizations struggle to recruit, hire, and retain cybersecurity talent, according to a Fortinet report, "CISO Ascends from Technologist to Strategic Business Enabler," which explores the skills gap.[2]

Addressing this gap requires a multi-pronged approach. Security knowledge needs to be more widely disseminated across the organization. Security and IT should be integrated, with cross-training between IT and security personnel. IT should also not be the only recruitment area for the security team: look across business units to identify potential candidates who bring experience of all types, from risk to finance to customer care to build out the security workforce.

To close the skills gap, we need to create a culture where people want to engage in the security business. To make the field more attractive, from frontline security workers to leaders, we need to increase the visibility of and influence of the CISO. They need to be considered an integral part of the C-suite and central to business success, not a cyber janitor to clean up problems or take the fall when a breach happens.

Although technical skills remain important, soft skills such as leadership, communications, planning, risk management, and strategy are just as vital. Such skills are especially critical for those in the CISO role who are leading security teams and communicating with the board.

We also need to make the field more diverse by recruiting more women as well as people of all backgrounds including race, ethnicity, orientation, and disability status. Further, we need to expand hiring efforts to recruit veterans, whose backgrounds position them as valued and committed employees.

Women are finally making some inroads in cybersecurity. In 2013, women held 11% of cybersecurity jobs; now women make up 24% of the cybersecurity workforce. While this improvement is positive news, more progress needs to be made, particularly since women make up half of the entire workforce.

Closing the diversity gap is not just a feel-good measure. Closing the diversity gap drives business success and change. To lower cyber risk, we need to lower the level of group think. Teams with diverse backgrounds and experiences can uncover new, creative solutions to problems. Women bring unique traits to leadership, problem-solving, and security. For example, female CISOs scored higher than their male counterparts in critical soft skills, including 46% higher in leadership and 150% higher in analytical skills.[3] These are important traits as we work to ensure that people and processes make effective, safe use of technology.

Finally, we need to generate excitement within the security field by creating programs that effectively promote the security field including mentoring, internships, and engagement with schools from college down to K–12.

CISOs can't lead without a knowledgeable staff. Chapter 5 outlines the extent of the skills and diversity gaps. It gives you strategies for attracting the resources you need, including ways to upskill people in your organization who, after all, already know your business.

Since this is the people section of this book, let's start with you, and equip you with context about what it means to be a CISO in the face of today's threats.

Notes

1. https://www.isc2.org/Research/Workforce-Study

2. https://www.fortinet.com/resources-campaign/ciso/the-ciso-ascends-from-technologist-to-strategic-business-enabler-2

3. https://www.fortinet.com/resources-campaign/ciso/the-ciso-ascends-from-technologist-to-strategic-business-enabler-2

1

From Technologist to Strategist

SANJU MISRA

AM GLAD THAT THIS BOOK IS BROKEN INTO THREE SECTIONS: people, process, and technology. There is so much we need to do in each area to have a successful information security program. I hope to engage you to reflect on your career in information security.

In this chapter, I will share my experience and observations on making the leap from technologist to CISO. This evolution wasn't easy at times, and I often met with challenges, but it has also been very rewarding.

The CISO is a trusted strategist who has a seat at the table, both internally, speaking to business leaders about risk and what keeps them up at night, as well as externally, speaking to the board of directors.

In these contexts, it's not important that you display your technical acumen. It is assumed you have weighed the technical considerations as part of your viewpoint. Rather, your ability to transcend technical explanations and frame issues in terms of business risk is what allows you to be heard, to be understood, and to be successful in protecting the enterprise at a level appropriate for the risk tolerance of the company.

A Path to CISO

If you asked a hundred information security and risk leaders how they got involved in the field, I'm sure you'd hear some interesting stories.

I never thought about an information security career early on. I was a biology major with an interest in what computers could do for the field, but not in programming. I helped fellow students with their essays and term papers by typing up their final presentations ... yup, on a trusty Smith-Corona.

9

A friend suggested I use the computer lab and try WordPerfect as a word processor to complete the final papers. Boy, it sure was easier to make updates and changes to documents compared to the typewriter.

When there was an opening to work part-time in the computer lab, I took it. The job made me learn more about how computers work by troubleshooting student questions about printing, using spreadsheets, and saving documents.

It wasn't until I had spent ten years after college at various IT jobs— including administering databases, providing end-user services, pulling network cables, upgrading and rebuilding PCs, and simple scripting—that I took my first role in information security.

I found out about a security engineer role when a large health insurer was looking to build out their consumer internet presence. A friend said I should meet the CISO and apply.

Eight years later, I left that company to take on the security leader role for the world's largest corporate treasury department in a Fortune 100 company.

Another eight years later (do you see a pattern to my tenure?), a recruiter from a large industrial gas company was looking for their first CISO after elevating the role internally. I had been with the company for six years before we merged with another large industrial gas company.

Okay, enough about my career path—let's talk about what CISOs do[1] in general terms. Our role shapes how we approach technical problems, our analytical skills, and the lens we use to view the cybersecurity world.

Almost a quarter of CISOs come from an IT background, with 56% having a Bachelor of Science degree. Of those who secured a graduate degree, 18% studied for an MBA. Top CISOs interviewed have stated the two most critical skill sets are information security and leadership. The backgrounds of the sixty-five (only 13%!) female CISOs[2] within the Fortune 500 are similar. They come from the same backgrounds and typically have spent more years in the same industry than their male counterparts. (See Chapter 5 for more information on the skills and diversity gap.)

Responsibilities of a CISO

While many join the information security field from IT, others come from audit, legal, risk, engineering, or business functions. Each area brings a valuable view to the risk picture. No matter which of these areas you come from, as long as you don't make decisions based entirely on your own experience, you will bring a more holistic view about what to prioritize. Stereotypically, a background in audit focuses on previous audit findings and compliance, whereas the business function may view security from a business enabler or cost avoidance perspective. All of these views are important to consider as you develop your security risk program.

There is an expectation that CISOs and their leadership teams have a wide range of IT experience to understand and speak the lingo with IT employees and make informed decisions. Having deep knowledge about information security alone is not enough to be a CISO. Strong leadership and communication skills are even more valuable. You must understand the organization's vision and strategy and create a security risk program aligned with business strategy. You will be expected to drive appropriate measures to ensure that information assets and technologies are safeguarded appropriately, depending on the type of data and exposure the system has. Resiliency is essential to discuss when creating a security program because inevitably incidents will happen and affect the business. Successful leaders help their businesses recover with limited business impact.

CISO Archetypes

The other day I was texting with a few CISO colleagues, and we started a video call, a scenario all too familiar in the days of the 2020 pandemic. We were talking about the fact that although there are many different personalities in our field, they are all able to succeed.

CISOs tend to fall into one of three buckets or archetypes, according to SecurityRoundtable.org:[3]

- The techie turned executive
- The enterprise security risk-focused thinker
- The "connect the dots" leader

So which one is the "correct" archetype? Actually, it doesn't matter whether you're a techie, a risk-focused thinker, or a politically and threat-savvy "connect the dots" leader. The fit of the particular archetype to the organization determines whether the company, the security organization, and, by extension, the CISO are successful. Each archetype brings their own strengths and approach.

The techie turned executive tends to work with or for the CIO, as more than half of all CISOs do today. A techie's strength is the ability to understand the technology and how it can best help reduce risk. The techie turned executive needs to broaden their approach and look beyond technology when working with business leaders to articulate risk.

The second archetype, the risk-focused thinker, aligns information security with business strategy. This leader understands the big picture and the business, as well as its risks. Because of the business and risk focus, these CISOs are increasingly reporting to the chief risk officer (CRO). According to consulting firm Korn Ferry, this shift is marked in the financial services sector because of increasing regulatory requirements around data privacy.[4]

The last archetype often comes from a government background and takes in the latest threats and geopolitical trends. Because of their experience and connections, they have a very broad view informed by the latest threats — as well as the threat actors behind them. Financial services and healthcare organizations are hiring more of these CISOs; in addition to their strong security background, they are savvy about regulatory issues.

What makes the archetype fit so challenging is that companies often don't know what they want from their CISOs, and CISOs aren't always clear about the kind of leaders they want to be. Because CISO responsibilities and concerns aren't the same from company to company and industry to industry, there is room to shape the role to best fit the strategic focus of the business. As a result, companies often look to the CISO to help define the role[5] as well as their security posture and program.

An incompatibility between cybersecurity executives and their organizations leads to burnout and contributes to high CISO turnover. According to research from the Enterprise Strategy Group, the average CISO lasts just two to four years.[6] If there's a mismatch, you'll see unhappy and unmotivated leaders who are prone to leaving the company sooner.

When a business is unsure of what they need, they may find out their current or recruited CISO is not a good fit for the company culture and risk profile. This scenario becomes crystal clear as you review CISO job descriptions. Such job descriptions often include technical duties like "create firewall rules," governance-focused elements like "create and maintain KPIs," and everything in between. CISO job descriptions are very different across industries as well as across organizations of different sizes and maturity levels.

There are some important red flags to look out for when you're looking a new role, according to CSO Online.[7]

For example, think hard before taking a role as a company's first CISO. Many first-time CISOs last only one year because the C-suite expects too much too soon, no matter how long the organization (and its infrastructure) has been around.

At the same time, as a new CISO, you might expect to have a healthy budget to work with, but the C-suite might not be ready to invest what you think they need to in order to address pre-existing issues. Anticipate possible conflicts around how secure you think the organization should be versus what the organization is willing to spend (see Chapter 6 to learn more about determining and framing issues relative to your organization's risk appetite).

On the positive side, being a company's first CISO can allow you to take the initiative and develop and influence the security risk program for an organization with the proper support. It could be the best role you've ever taken in your career!

The reporting structure is another issue. Today most CISOs report to the CIO, but not every CIO is a strong leader. If a CISO reports to a CIO who is not a strong leader, the CIO may look for an excuse to replace the CISO. If you see this dynamic, it could be time to look for another job or at least consider ways to strengthen your partnership with the CIO gradually.

Look out for organizations that want a CISO mainly for window-dressing. These companies want a CISO to assure the board and their customers that all is well with their data and compliance. In fact, they aren't willing to make necessary changes. These companies can't keep a CISO around, so you'll see many job openings at these organizations. Their CISOs leave out of sheer frustration. They often feel they are just checking the box on compliance requirements, and their ideas for a strong cybersecurity program are always stalled because the budget or resources are never available. In such roles, you will never be running a sound cybersecurity program.

Rock-star CISOs are a tough act to follow because the organization really wanted to keep their existing CISO. Expect comparisons with the previous CISO. This can be very frustrating, because every CISO has a unique brand and identity—yet their identity may never be recognized because of constant comparison with the prior CISO.

If you decide to take such a role, keep the prior CISO's programs in place. Over time, you can slowly modify and change the cybersecurity program by bringing your own personality and security philosophy to the enterprise.

Evolution of the CISO Role

As mentioned, the majority of CISOs report to the CIO. Forming a strong, collaborative relationship with the CIO whether you're a subordinate of the

CIO or outside IT in the risk, legal, or audit group is key. I'll be bold and say you won't be successful if you can't influence the IT function. Without sincere respect and alignment between the CIO and the CISO, organizations may devolve into a tech turf war that creates roadblocks to success.

With the increasing demand to embed security into all digital transformation processes and a move to more decentralized structures and business unit autonomy, the information security function is evolving to meet shifts in the business climate.

Instead of just protecting the enterprise, the CISO role has evolved to enable fundamental changes in the business environment. This means the focus has shifted to the security officer being a business enabler. The CISO's department is no longer the "Department of No" but rather the "Department of Know."[8]

The COVID-19 pandemic forced CISOs to meet pressing business needs and to reimagine ways to enable the business to go on. Many employees started to work from home, and that meant the security risk model needed to adapt.

It was especially challenging. How could existing tools securely handle the increased bandwidth, personally owned devices, and the sharing of home and corporate networks? More importantly, security folks needed to understand what teams and business employees were doing in 2020 to get their jobs at work (and home) done.

If we don't provide a simple secure method for the business to complete a task, people will go around the controls each and every time, and that introduces more risk. We as a security community need to continue building solutions and tactics that enable employees to work securely. Being a business enabler is the way to do that.

Consider the case where a company restricts access to file-sharing websites. Despite these restrictions, many employees need to upload documents to these sites for regulators, customers, vendor partners, or corporate functions. So if you are a representative of the Department of No and don't explain why you have the policy, the employee will upload those company documents while off the company VPN, on their home network, or via their home computer. It would be better to provide employees with the ability to do their job and not have to circumvent the controls you put in place.

It's important to realize that what made you a technical lead or subject matter expert won't get you a seat at the table with business leaders and the board of directors. CISOs are not the most technical resource in the room.

Instead, you need to be seen more as the CFO of cybersecurity. Like a CFO, you'll need soft skills and the ability to influence and communicate effectively. Stop speaking in technical jargon. Speak the language of the business leader. Board members and the office of the chairperson are used to hearing risk and financial impact presentations, and you have to frame cybersecurity risk in the same way.

Watch out for security operations terms or metrics. Each metric should be followed by "so what?" If you can't answer that question in a nontechnical way, remove the metric or adapt it. Think about old-school business risk calculations. What is the chance of the event multiplied by the impact of that event? Risk definitions don't change, even for the cybersecurity world.

Technical Strengths Versus Security Officer Strengths

Many of us came to our careers as subject matter experts in a particular technical field. If you are like us, you were the "go-to" person for that area of expertise. You built trust with others, and they reached out to you for solutions to tough technical problems. You may be used to addressing multiple audiences.

If you have those technical strengths, start positioning yourself today for the CISO role. Take on the task or challenge no one wants ... you know the one. It's the one that's considered too big, too hard, or where multiple people failed in the past. Increase your visibility to business leaders. Make sure their perception of you is extremely positive because perception becomes reality. Demonstrate your influence in getting work done. This is key in the CISO role as you typically don't have direct responsibilities in the various areas you need to change in order to be successful. You'll need those influencing skills.[9]

It's important to build up relationships across the organization including with the legal, human resources, privacy, digital, and risk departments. All of these areas have inputs into the risk posture for the company, and you'll be working with them more as you become the CISO.

When you have the opportunity to present to senior business leaders or the board of directors, remember that you are the cybersecurity subject matter expert. Use your limited time to educate them and provide a risk view that is in alignment with other business risks. Be prepared to defend your position. Use nontechnical terms. Talk about risk. This requires you to know about the business drivers, the risk appetite, and the top risks the company tracks. Many board members also serve on other company boards so they may be versed in the subject. If they see another company approaching risk in a certain way, be prepared for questions about whether you're doing enough or why you took another approach.

Cybersecurity risk is similar to purchasing insurance. You invest in helping the business hedge against the devastating effects of cybercrimes. While external cybersecurity insurance may be purchased, there is an assumption that the CISO has the risks identified and controls put into place. If there is an incident, detect and respond quickly. Be resilient in terms of business impact.

Be ready to answer the following questions prior to speaking to the board. What is the organization's cyber risk level? What are the organization's top risks? How is the organization's risk posture trending? Are the risks going up or down? Is the organization's level of cybersecurity spending appropriate for the company? Be prepared to request support and funding where needed. Use a pragmatic and straightforward approach for funding requests, as opposed to crying wolf or assuming you won't get funding.

Senior leaders are accustomed to applying metrics and watching trends. What are meaningful metrics for cybersecurity risk? Think about how to explain intrusion attempts. How would you explain metrics like the mean time to detect attacks? How will you explain the risks in supply chain and vendor management? Lastly, how will you quantify how your organization measures up compared with its peers?

When approaching metrics,[10] be transparent about performance. Use economically focused results based on easy-to-understand methods. Benchmark your metrics against your peers or your industry. Make your presentation decision-oriented so that the board can provide oversight of management's decisions, including resource allocation, security controls, and cyber insurance.

When you look at your metrics, try to stay away from security operational or shock-and-awe metrics. You know the type: the ones that state the company blocked hundreds of emails every day, stopped more than 500 intrusion attempts on the external perimeter, or 90% of systems have the latest anti-malware protection.

Again, ask "so what?" at the end of that statement. Is that a lot? A little? Should we block more or less? What was it last month or quarter? How is the metric trending? Why do we care? Are we doing enough? What are other companies seeing or doing in this space? Think of those questions as you're putting together your metrics and consider the sustainability of metrics. Will you be able to provide these metrics on a regular basis without spending countless weeks gathering the information?

With opportunities growing in many organizations, we still need to keep the pressure on companies and on ourselves. Many companies see the CISO role as an "IT thing" or function. I am optimistic that over time, we will see the CISO role elevated in more companies, outside the financial services industry, similar to other C-suite roles like chief marketing officer, chief digital officer, chief risk officer, and chief privacy officer. This will happen as cybersecurity is seen as essential to the proper functioning of the enterprise. Fortunately or unfortunately, depending on your perspective, the current threat landscape is increasing the respect for the office of the CISO.

Notes

1.   https://blogvaronis2.wpengine.com/ciso-skills/
2.   https://www.varonis.com/blog/female-cybersecurity-leaders/
3.   https://www.securityroundtable.org/ciso-archetypes/
4.   https://www.kornferry.com/content/dam/kornferry/docs/article-migration/The_Rise_of_the_Chief_Information_Security_Officer.pdf
5.   https://searchsecurity.techtarget.com/feature/Which-type-of-CISO-are-you-Company-fit-matters
6.   https://searchsecurity.techtarget.com/feature/CISO-position-burnout-causes-high-churn-rate
7.   https://www.csoonline.com/article/3166061/a-cisos-guide-to-avoiding-certain-ciso-jobs.html
8.   https://www.cshub.com/executive-decisions/articles/the-department-of-no-becomes-the-department-of-know
9.   https://garfinkleexecutivecoaching.com/books/getting-ahead
10. https://blog.nacdonline.org/posts/getting-the-right-cybersecurity-metrics-and-reports-for-your-board

SANJU MISRA

Sanju Misra is currently VP and CISO of Alnylam
Pharmaceuticals where she focuses on maturing the
information security and risk program. Her role is
safeguarding Alnylam's confidential information, intellectual property, and
information operational technology systems as well as meeting technology
compliance and regulatory requirements. Prior to joining Alnylam, Sanju was
CISO of Praxair/Linde Industrial Gases for seven years.

Sanju has over twenty-three years of information security experience in the
healthcare, financial, and chemicals industries including roles at GE Capital and
Aetna Health Insurance.

Sanju is passionate about growing the cybersecurity talent pipeline by
mentoring students in cybersecurity and STEM careers. In her spare time, she
volunteers at an adult literacy agency as well as a shelter for women and children.

2

Communicating with the Board

MARIANNE BAILEY

CHIEVING EFFECTIVE COMMUNICATION CAN BE ONE OF THE most difficult tasks. People face this challenge as they talk past each other often in everyday lives because one party assumes the other has the same background, biases, and interests. This problem is no different when communicating with boards of directors.

In order to overcome this communication gap, it is critical to understand the mission of the board, to speak in their language, and to clearly articulate why they should care about whatever it is you are telling them. The communication gap is significant because leaders and employees operate in a more tactical and— in the case of cybersecurity—a more technical environment all day, every day.

Board members operate in a more strategic and a much broader environment. I can't even count the times I've heard technical people venting their frustration after a board briefing. "They don't understand our business," they say. "We need more technical board members. They need to spend more time understanding what we do."

All the blame is put on the board. Meanwhile the board members see the employee as unprepared, unable to communicate the issues in a strategic manner, and unable to help the board members see the impact. At the end of the day, the company is less effective because the employees cannot relay the concerns to the board and the board members do not understand the issues and thus cannot advise or take action.

The Board

The function of the board—and this is true for many senior committees—is to evaluate the overall strategy and the organization's progression toward that strategy. Their agendas are packed and diverse. The board will often be comprised of the chairman of the board, the CEO, the CFO, general counsel, and external experts. Topics range from the organization's financials, investments, and overall business strategy to HR issues (leadership, talent challenges, diversity numbers) and legal and regulatory issues. Chartered with overseeing everything from financial success, prospective investments, and culture to staffing issues, boards are not often given abundant time to focus on one topic. Communication to the board must be presented in a clear, crisp, and easily understood format.

Speak Their Language

The first significant challenge is speaking the same language. Technical people, including those in cybersecurity, speak their own unique language. They have a very difficult time discussing their programs at a high level with context that boards and senior leaders understand.

As a leader of many technology organizations, I experienced this challenge from my first leadership position all the way up to my positions as the cybersecurity lead at NSA and the principal director/deputy CIO for cybersecurity in the Pentagon. Whether technical staff or leaders were briefing me or whether I was preparing staff to brief top boards and committees in the Pentagon, Congress, or the White House, I would spend significant time pulling pertinent information from a fifty-page briefing. I would rarely see a clear and concise presentation. Individuals include far too much information and do not articulate their message. I would ask them, "What are you trying to tell me, or your senior audience? What do you want from me, or them?" It is very important to understand your audience and tailor your message to that audience in a way that resonates with their responsibilities.

Preparing for the Board Meeting

Do your homework. Be able to answer these questions:

- Who are the board members? What are their backgrounds? Are there members of the board who will be allies for my program? Is there an opportunity to share information with them ahead of the board meeting? If so, take every opportunity to meet one-on-one with them to explain your program and your issues. You will find that even one or two board members who become advocates will be extremely valuable.

- What are the company's big strategic pushes?

- Is my position in line with my leadership? You never want to oppose your leadership in a board meeting. Understand that your leaders have many issues they are working on and yours may not currently be the top priority. It is not worth damaging the trust relationship, and it demonstrates a lack of understanding of their position.

- How does my program impact the company's culture, reputation, and cost? Why should they care? How can they help?

- Are there pros and cons? Can I list them in a way that will resonate with the board?

- Is my message clear and succinct?

Keep It Direct, Crisp, and Simple

It's not the Gettysburg Address, and it's not a graduate-level course. One of my favorite quotes comes from Mark Twain: "I didn't have time to write a short letter, so I wrote a long one instead." Your time with the board is often very short. It is important to craft a clear and crisp message. I have seen many fifty-page briefings prepared for senior-level boards. Written papers have an executive summary for a reason; that is all most senior-level individuals will read! Your board brief should be that executive summary.

State the purpose of your briefing immediately. Don't leave them guessing. "Our reputation is at risk if we do not improve the security posture of our company. Our competitors have invested in state-of-the-art security. Our customers are vulnerable. We could be held liable if their data is breached. The average cost of a breach today is $$$. The cost of our remediation program is $$. These are our steps; this is our timeline." Give them high-level, impactful, data-driven information that they can now use to make a risk decision.

Don't assume they know your subject, and don't try to teach them details they do not need to know. You will lose them in the process, and they'll lose your message. I will always remember one of the most challenging proposals I had to prepare.

I was in a cybersecurity position in the Pentagon. We had an opportunity to obtain funding for a program we wanted to kick off. The CIO asked me to come to his office. I walked across the hall, and he sat across from me at his conference table. He explained that we had opportunity to obtain support from the Secretary of Defense. "You have one paragraph to explain the program, why he should care, and what it will cost and you cannot use one technical word," he said. He told me to dictate, and he would capture it. If I explained anything in a technical manner—words like *enterprise, interoperability, automation, advanced analytics*—he would give me a verbal buzzer. It was quite a challenge, and it makes me laugh to this day. We were successful, but it was not an easy paragraph, and I received that verbal buzzer more often than I would have thought.

I have found that analogies are incredibly useful. Recently, I was asked by board members why it is important for their company to mitigate all of their critical vulnerabilities. Why isn't 80% good enough? I used a very simple house-windows-and-doors analogy. If you put state-of-the-art locks and monitoring on all of your windows and doors except the back door, which you leave totally unprotected, you have not done much to protect your house. Add to that the bad guy who can scan your house before arriving to determine what protections you have on all of your windows and doors. You have just given that bad guy a road map to enter your house undetected. Immediately, the board members got it. I did not have to explain what a bad guy could do if they didn't upgrade a specific OS or patch a specific vulnerability. It didn't matter. All that mattered is the bad guy could get in, and 80% mitigation is not good enough.

Working Directly for the Board: The Ultimate Case Study

After 9/11 I was asked to set up the first joint DoD/IC organization, the Unified Cross Domain Management Office (UCDMO). The UCDMO was established to solve the problem of cross-domain information sharing among all of DoD, including our troops overseas and the intelligence communities. There was no holistic strategy nor was there anyone in the lead. I used the analogy of kiddie soccer with everyone running toward the ball (yes, I used this analogy with the board). It resonated very well because I could provide example after example of duplication, lack of strategy, and agencies not playing their roles.

The UCDMO was a "volunteer" organization that directly reported to the board and no one else. The board was co-chaired by the Director of National Intelligence CIO and the Department of Defense CIO. Each agency and service had a three-star general as a board member. Not only did I constantly have to convince the individual board members to staff my organization, but I also had to continuously provide evidence of success and therefore of value for the organization to continue to be funded. The board met every quarter for a two-hour status report meeting and annually to appraise the success and decide on the continuation of the office. I knew I could not rely on these meetings alone to communicate the work we were doing and the support we needed.

The Power of One-on-One Meetings

In order to be successful, I met with every board member individually, weekly or biweekly. I made it a point to get to know them and to understand their role and their specific interest. I was able to grow this organization from two people to fifty in less than a year and expand our budget significantly. When there was a tough issue—and we had plenty of them—I knew who to lobby, who would provide advice to make sure I thoroughly researched the issue, and who would support me at the board meeting. While that individual often changed from issue to issue, I cannot overemphasize how much a fellow board member can sway the position of the board or even calm concerns of other board members. I rarely was surprised by any member's position, and that enabled me to prepare for that position ahead of time.

During my one-on-one meetings, there were times my thirty-minute slot was cut to five. Sometimes it would be a walk down the hall to their next meeting. I learned very quickly that my communication, my elevator pitch, or my first slide needed to be the whole story. I learned the value of being clear, concise, and direct. What did I need from them? Why should they care? How is my proposal going to solve the problem? What are the risks? Why is my approach the best solution? Why do I need additional resources, and when do I need them?

A few of the board members were technologists, but most of them were not. Explaining a technical issue in their language became critical. This included topics like timelines, costs, risks, and impact to the broader organization. In my case, that meant the entire Department of Defense, the intelligence community, and most important the military and civilians who needed the information wherever they were in the world and on whatever network they operated. Speak to the board in company mission and business terms and explain how your solution advances the business.

Get to Know Your Board

The time you spend understanding the individuals who comprise your board will be time very well spent. If you familiarize yourself with their backgrounds and why they were selected as a board member, you will develop a presentation that resonates with them. When they ask questions, you'll better understand their concerns based on their focus and background. Be clear and concise; know the information, but don't present every technical detail. Speak their language and state up front why your ask is important to the business. Do your homework by socializing your presentation internally, ensuring you have leadership support, as well as externally if you can obtain individual meetings with board members. If you build knowledgeable allies and tailor your conversation to the interests and priorities of your board, chances of a successful outcome will greatly improve.

MARIANNE BAILEY

Marianne Bailey is a partner at Guidehouse who leads the Advanced Solutions Cybersecurity practice to provide strategies and solutions that enable Guidehouse clients to develop and sustain cyber resilience to mitigate cybersecurity risks against current and emerging threats.

Marianne brings over thirty-five years of experience across the Department of Defense (DoD), intelligence community, and civil government sectors. She served as Deputy National Manager for National Security Systems (NSS) and Senior Cybersecurity Executive for the National Security Agency where she was directly responsible for systems across the government containing classified and sensitive information. She also served as both Principal Deputy for Cybersecurity and Deputy Chief Information Security Officer (DCISO) and Department of Defense CIO. She received the Distinguished Executive Presidential Rank Award, the highest government civilian recognition, for her contributions to national security.

Marianne has led US cyber policy and technology initiatives internationally and is well known for her global leadership in cyber. She has received many awards recognizing her efforts, including the Office of the Secretary of Defense Medal for Exceptional Civilian Service, FedScoop's Top Women in IT, and WashingtonExec's Top 25 Cyber Executives to Watch (2020).

Marianne earned a BS in engineering from the University of Maryland and a master's in resourcing the national strategy (economics) from the Industrial College of the Armed Forces, National Defense University. She is a graduate of the NSA Senior Leadership Development Program (2003–2007), the Harvard Executive Leadership Development Program, and the Executive Leadership at the Peak Program.

3 | Building a Culture of Security

SUSAN KOSKI

W HAT DOES IT MEAN TO BUILD A CULTURE OF SECURITY IN a business? All too often, the security organization is associated with the voice of "no." Given the pace of the digital economy and the business need to be proactive for competitive advantage, security must be an embedded part of all solutions. Instead of saying "no," a security organization must be able to say "yes" while detailing the operating conditions that enable that yes. If security is seen as the voice of "no," then serious security risks may not be identified, placing the business and company at a greater risk. The security organization must evolve to become a trusted advisor to the business.

The pinnacle of achievement is when, instead of being avoided, the security group is actively sought out for advice. Businesses reach this pinnacle when the culture of security is so embedded that when new or changing initiatives are presented, security is woven in throughout the design, build, and implementation. Without this embedded culture of security, solutions will be delivered without the proper controls, which can lead to breaches and to customer and shareholder dissatisfaction. The CISO's job—and everyone's job—is to enable the business to drive their car as fast as they need to with the proper safety measures such as brakes, air bags, and seatbelts in place to attain an acceptable safety level.

Depending on where the security organization is relative to maturity, this can seem daunting. If approached with relationship management, communication, and awareness, it can be a fun journey where everyone at the company, not just those in the security group, has security as their job. The security group must build trust and deliver business-enabling capabilities. These capabilities can be both tactical—keeping the lights on—as well as creating capacity within your security group to get a seat at the strategy table with business leaders.

As a CISO, this is an incredible opportunity to win the hearts and minds of your constituents so that they become security advocates. The ultimate success is when your phone is ringing and your email is filled with requests from the business. Always take those calls, answer those emails, and listen. Once you have the audience, make sure that you sustain and keep those customers because winning them back is harder than winning them over.

This will not be easy, but when it is achieved, security has a consistent seat at the table and is viewed as a valued business consultant. Now, let's get started on our journey!

The Building Blocks of the Journey

Cultural change must occur in tandem with the growing maturity of the security program. This is important because organizational awareness should build as the maturity of the security program increases. As the foundational elements for maturity are achieved, security can evolve from alignment to risk tolerance to consultancy. To evolve to consultancy, there must be mature services to offer so that during the consultancy, risk-aware advice can be offered that is aligned with the risk of the business objective.

What are the building blocks for the journey to a high-performing security organization that has the trust, respect, and ear of the business? Figure 3-1 shows the evolution from building a foundation to becoming a trusted advisor. The rest of this chapter describes the building stages of the security program and their alignment with building a culture of security awareness.

The cultural elements of security include:

- Leadership and organizational support
- Communications
- Measuring effectiveness
- Measuring engagement
- Relationship management

In Figure 3-1, these cultural elements are in *italic text.*

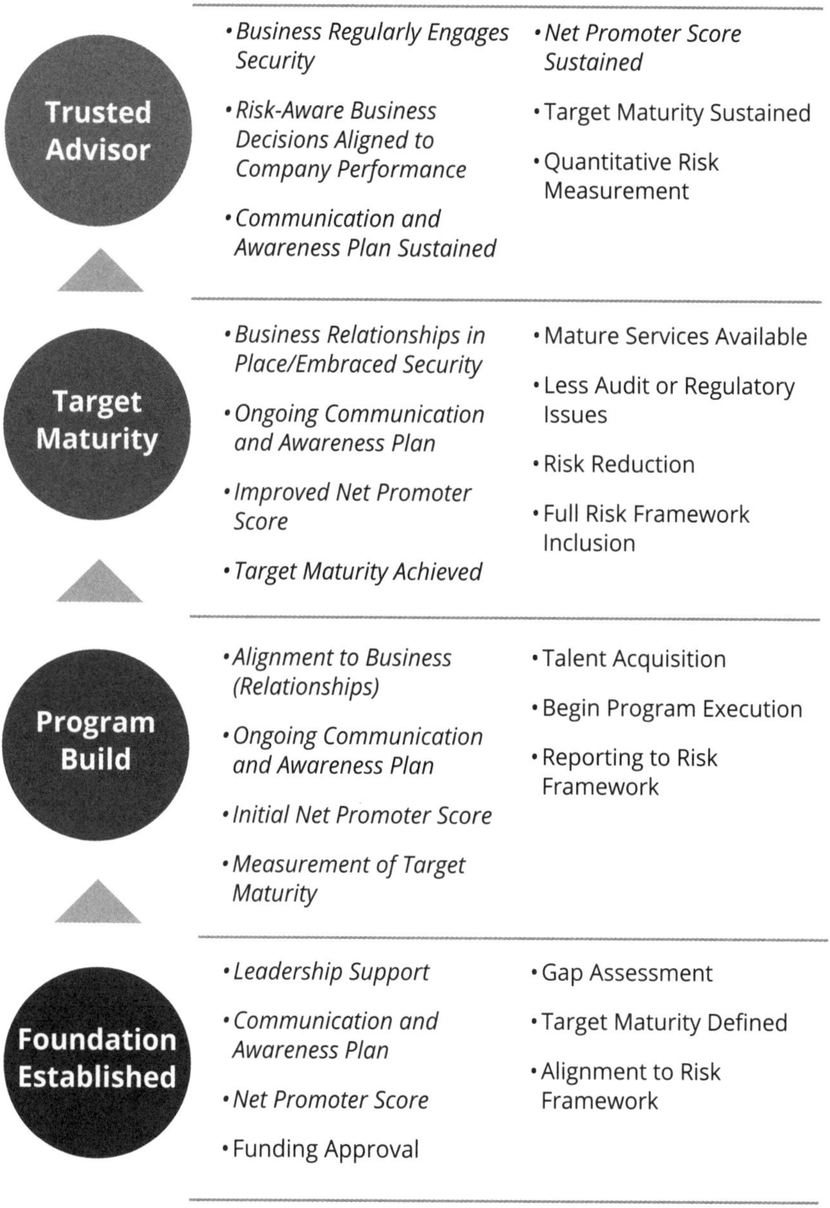

Trusted Advisor

- *Business Regularly Engages Security*
- *Risk-Aware Business Decisions Aligned to Company Performance*
- *Communication and Awareness Plan Sustained*
- *Net Promoter Score Sustained*
- *Target Maturity Sustained*
- Quantitative Risk Measurement

Target Maturity

- *Business Relationships in Place/Embraced Security*
- *Ongoing Communication and Awareness Plan*
- *Improved Net Promoter Score*
- *Target Maturity Achieved*
- Mature Services Available
- Less Audit or Regulatory Issues
- Risk Reduction
- Full Risk Framework Inclusion

Program Build

- *Alignment to Business (Relationships)*
- *Ongoing Communication and Awareness Plan*
- *Initial Net Promoter Score*
- *Measurement of Target Maturity*
- Talent Acquisition
- Begin Program Execution
- Reporting to Risk Framework

Foundation Established

- *Leadership Support*
- *Communication and Awareness Plan*
- *Net Promoter Score*
- Funding Approval
- Gap Assessment
- Target Maturity Defined
- Alignment to Risk Framework

Figure 3-1. The evolution of a culture of security awareness

Program and Cultural Foundation

Establishing a foundation for the security program is critical. Even if there is already a program in place, revisit these foundational areas to ensure the foundation is strong and includes needed elements to achieve broader cultural awareness.

Leadership Support

Support from executive management is requisite to obtaining outcomes aligned with corporate risk tolerance that achieve the target maturity. Organizations follow their leaders, so this support is crucial to enable the willingness to provide the funding to achieve required changes. Organizational willingness is very closely tied to understanding the perceived tone and tenor of the security organization and what it delivers to the company.

Communication and Awareness Plan

A communication plan must be combined with an awareness plan. Security must communicate their current posture and programs and ask for input from the business. This plan should include where, when, and how the security program should be communicated. Consider not only how the security organization will provide the business awareness but also how the group will gain awareness about the business and the forums to participate in to do so.

Net Promoter Score

Net promoter score is commonly used to measure customer loyalty. An understanding of the perception of security from revenue and non-revenue-generating parts of the business is necessary to establish a baseline of the opportunities to change the awareness of both the security team and the entire business. Security leaders can often be perceived as lacking business acumen or empathy. Measuring the perception of the security organization is one of the first steps in building a culture of security awareness.

To establish a methodology for capturing the net promoter score, security teams should engage with the marketing, communications, and human resources departments. These groups can serve as a starting point for grassroots support for security and become an extension of the security team. Ensure that security listens to and embraces the suggestions of these teams in order to learn from both the promoters and the detractors.

Funding Approval

Funding for key personnel demonstrates leadership support to build the program to attain the level of needed maturity. Often, technical personnel are not the best consultants, so thoughtful consideration must be given in the hiring process to find subject matter leaders who are great communicators. These leaders must be able to understand the needs of the business, solutions available, and solutions needed. Security leaders must excel at storytelling in the language of the business.

Gap Assessment

Assessing security capabilities for gaps in both functionality and staffing is critical because it is necessary to have the right capabilities and consistently deliver those capabilities. If the building blocks of the program are not available, the security team will not be able to deliver a service to the business to enable its safety and security.

First, take stock of what security capabilities exist and measure them against an industry framework. What capabilities are missing? Are they critical to support the business? Are these the right capabilities, and are there opportunities to streamline solutions to leapfrog in maturity? Instead of multiple best-of-breed solutions that do not integrate, how do you migrate to platform-level integrated stacks that work together seamlessly to deliver the capability? Build out the plan to enable these capabilities and prioritize it based not only on risk reduction but also on the value that is delivered—and perceived—by the business.

Target Maturity Defined

From the gap assessment, attain agreement from leadership on the risks and the acceptable security maturity level for your firm. Once in agreement, ensure that the security program has ways to convey accomplishments in terms that are meaningful to the business.

Alignment to Risk Framework

Each company has various methods by which they measure risk, typically in line with an enterprise risk management framework. Ensure that the security program has controls aligned to this framework, measured at the business unit level. Also, establish working sessions with people in the risk organization. They can be incredible advocates and assist in spreading the word about the security program.

Program Build and Cultural Engagement

The next phase involves building your security program while driving cultural engagement.

Alignment to Business (Relationships)

Relationship management is required throughout because cultural change cannot be enabled from the top down or bottom up—it must be woven into all levels of the organization. In this phase, determine if you can align dedicated personnel to the business and technology teams. If there are dedicated personnel, assign key leaders to have fireside chats with those teams. Be prepared with materials that describe the security mission and vision while also listening intently for business problems and how security could help to address them. With this knowledge, the security team will also gain insight into how to measure business outcomes and key results to further tell the security story. As the program builds, seek to establish business security champions—personnel who can be your ambassadors to carry the security message to the business.

Ongoing Communication and Awareness Plan

To be effective at driving program maturity, the security team must communicate the message in appropriate forums such as business steering committees, advisory groups, and councils. Hire appropriate personnel who are not technologists to help craft the messages in business meaningful ways with clear examples that convey the message about the value security brings to the organization. Besides the business forums, work with your colleagues in risk to identity risk forums to share information about the security program and seek advice. As part of these forums, establish a metric about the consulting engagements that security is asked to participate in. As the program matures, they should turn from tactical requests to strategic requests for programs.

Educating employees about their responsibilities is one of the most important parts of your program build. These programs can utilize either a carrot or stick approach, and possibly both. Start by making the program personal—offer tips to utilize with home computers to enhance the online safety of employees' children and even that of their aging parents.[1]

People want to do the right thing. Start with the basics and educate personnel in three to five areas and then measure their successes. Encourage positive behavior in reporting issues—celebrate those successes with your company's rewards program and articles on the intranet spotlighting an individual who did the right thing. These individuals will tell ten to twenty more people what they did to receive praise, continuing to spread security awareness. Throughout the program build, measure reporting of issues to the security team. If done right, you should see an increase in reporting over time.

Spend time having fireside chats with the frontline personnel—those in the help desk or customer care centers. Provide insight on things that do not seem right. Act on reports from these teams because these reports can often be the first sign of a possible issue. Praise these folks for their work; make sure their managers know about and reward positive behavior through your company's rewards program for reporting security issues.

For all employees, play games! Yes, I said play games. Choose games that encourage the players to learn trivia about security. Do crossword puzzles and play trivia games; then reward people with prizes. Remember: those who are rewarded will tell someone, and they will tell someone, and so on. As an example, have a top-ten set of questions about security and give hints throughout October, which is National Security Awareness month. Give a prize for the first person who answers all the trivia questions correctly. For another example, host a session where the security group demonstrates capabilities and provides security advice. Give a prize to the individual who gets the most security booths stamped on their card, like many conferences do.

Of course, building a culture of security cannot be all fun and games. A consequences model, aligned with human resources, is needed for certain behaviors. For example, if an employee has privileged access to systems but abuses that privilege, what are the consequences, given the severity of the misuse of trust? And how do you differentiate between deliberate abuse and problems that arise when employees are in a hurry and skip security steps?

Lastly, do not forget about customers—work with your business lines to understand their customers' net promoter scores and find out what customers care about in terms of security. You can then connect those findings to the security program, and the rationale for those measures will resonate in terms of customer satisfaction. This metric will tie your security program to a customer trust score, and as the program matures, the customer trust score will increase.

Initial Net Promoter Score

In this program build phase, take the initial measurement of the score of the security program—from all levels of the organization. Use this as input to tailor messages about program success and as insight into the best ways to engage with employees for security awareness. Leave room for open-ended questions about what is being done well and where there is opportunity for growth. Share this score and tie it to program metrics on engagement as discussed earlier.

Measurement of Target Maturity

Once you have selected a framework to measure maturity, incorporate reporting on the program into risk and business forums. Building on those relationships, seek advice on how to connect maturity improvements into illustrations of business value. This is the start of establishing metrics that matter—meaningful to describe risk and to communicate to the board and to the business. Metrics and reporting need to be tailored to the audience and should be somewhat distinct for each one. Explain why and how these are important to enable the business.

Talent Acquisition

Depending on the funding available, ensure that you staff the most important functions and seek traditional and nontraditional backgrounds for your staffing. Interview for skill as well as cultural fit in the company and find personnel who can speak the language of the business.

Begin Program Execution

Develop the key tenets of program execution and report them to necessary constituents. Have the key messages and the mission and vision of the organization ready to share with risk committees, forums, and business meetings. Find ways to tie the messages into the culture of the company and communicate how the program raises security awareness for employees and customers.

Reporting to Risk Framework

Be totally transparent about the overall status of the program. Show how the program is improving the effectiveness of security. Measurements are likely to be mainly qualitative.

Target Maturity and Cultural Enlightenment

In this phase of the program, the organization achieves the target maturity level and can offer mature services. Continued work is needed so that the culture of security permeates the organization.

Business Relationships in Place (Security Embraced)

At this stage, the business should mostly be reaching out to security for advice on key projects and initiatives. Continue to nurture the relationships and hold fireside chats, leveraging information attained to tie target maturity to business value. Teach your direct reports to develop peer relationships at their level. Have your leaders take a similar approach for fireside chats and listen to feedback. Make sure that the story explains the trade-offs between the user experience and security and how an appropriate balance can be maintained and understood. Lastly show the awareness metrics and their ties to customer net promoter scores.

Ongoing Communication and Awareness Plan

Continue the communication efforts during this phase. Upgrade your internal materials to show the maturity level attained and how it provides outcomes and key results for the business and the customers. Make sure that this is communicated at all levels of the organization. Highlight individuals who have reported security issues and show how that led to better outcomes for customers and the company. Provide industry examples of behavior that did not achieve the desired outcomes and show how the security program at your firm would change that negative outcome.

Improved Net Promoter Score

The net promoter score should continue to improve from the initial rating. At this point, regular net promoter scores should be collected, calculated, and leveraged to determine if there is a gap in the program or where additional information could be provided to the business to show how that perceived gap is being addressed.

Target Maturity Achieved and Mature Services Available

Achieving the target maturity means that you have mature security services to offer for challenging problems that solve business needs.

Fewer Audit or Regulatory Issues

With the target maturity, there should be fewer risk issues that take time away from more strategic capabilities. The best part about this is that the time recovered can be invested in greater efficiency and innovation—what I call "effovation."

Full Risk Framework Inclusion

Governance and risk management are integrated within the risk forum to discuss and determine the right risk decisions—security awareness is now woven into the fabric of the company. Metrics should matter to drive risk conversations and mainly be focused on quantitative measures at this stage.

Reaching Trusted Advisor

At the level of trusted advisor, the elements already established have a much heavier influence on maintaining a culture of security awareness. This does not mean the work is done; on the contrary, maintaining this level once achieved requires ongoing effort.

Business Regularly Engages Security

Security awareness has been reached, and security is a trusted advisor to solve complex business problems. Continue to permeate the organization and align all security staff to understand business problems.

Risk-Aware Business Decisions Aligned to Company Performance

Businesses are less likely to just accept risk without understanding the key facts about the risk. The security team is adept at explaining risk and what that means to the bottom line as well as various elements of the company's risk framework. Security risks can be combined with reputational, financial, and litigious risks.

Communication and Awareness Plan Sustained

Now that you have attained cultural engagement, what can you do to continually maintain engagement enthusiasm? Lean into research and talk with peers about additional methods to keep the spark of awareness alive.

Net Promoter Score Sustained

Maintain the net promoter score and set goals to improve this score alongside the customer net promoter scores. Ensure this is woven into scorecards where the team shares insight into why scores are rising or falling and what is being done about it.

Target Maturity Sustained

Achieving target maturity took an incredible amount of work. Do not lose sight of continuing to maintain and improve the maturity. Ensure improvements deliver value for a business problem, and don't sacrifice good for perfect.

Quantitative Risk Measurement

Metrics matter and at this stage are objectives and key results (OKR)[2] focused. These new objectives for the security program are ambitious, and the results should be easily measurable with an easy-to-follow scale. Most often, these goals will not be realistically attainable because they are designed to be ambitious to spur people to think bigger. OKRs can help teams focus on bigger bets above what anyone may have thought possible—continuing the effovation journey.

Effovation should reduce busywork, sometimes called ClickOps, allowing knowledge workers to focus on more complex problems—and in fact fail while doing so. Leaders should celebrate failures and what was learned from failure because those failures will drive greater wins. Leaders should also celebrate that knowledge workers have a desire to contribute and be recognized for being allowed to develop cool new ideas.

Conclusion

This framework outlines how security program maturity aligns with weaving a culture of security awareness throughout an organization. The work will be tough, but the rewards are incredible. In the end, your email will be full, and your phone won't stop ringing—because you and your team may be the most sought-after people in the company.[3]

Notes

1. https://www.pcmag.com/news/cybersecurity-training-try-the-carrot-instead-of-the-stick
2. https://www.whatmatters.com/articles/the-origin-story/
3. https://atlassian.com/blog/productivity/5-questions-about-motivation-with-daniel-pink

SUSAN KOSKI

Susan is an executive security leader who achieves a business balance of security and risk management. She has a record of rebuilding programs and developing highly functional teams. Susan also re-engineers processes and technology for efficiency and innovation (effovation). Susan is Senior VP and CISO at PNC and has held executive security positions including Managing Director of Technology Risk Management at BNY Mellon, CISO at Synovus, and Chief Data Protection Officer at Aetna.

Susan has an enduring focus on inspiring teams to reach their highest potential. She creates these effovation opportunities through a spirit of continuous learning and development to fully utilize investments while allowing for creativity for complex issues.

Susan holds a BS in electrical engineering from the University of Pittsburgh and an MBA from Duquesne University. Susan is CISO Executive Network Advisory Council member, Chair of the BITS Security Steering Committee, and a Governing Body member of the Evanta Pittsburgh CISO program.

4

Who Is Behind the Evolving Threat Landscape?

JENNY MENNA

T HE CYBER THREAT LANDSCAPE IS COMPLEX AND CONSTANTLY changing, and it can be difficult for even the most avid practitioner to keep up. Malware and ransomware variants morph and are renamed constantly by their creators. The question we will ask in this chapter is, who is behind the threats we face?

While cyberattacks leverage complex technologies, people are at the root of every successful breach or incident. Machines don't write malware and exploits; humans do. These attacks support their objectives. Those objectives vary widely.

There are malicious outsiders, from nation-states to criminals to hacktivists. But insiders—people inside your organization—are also often part of the problem.

We sometimes see malicious insiders, people who intentionally sabotage their employers for revenge or sell their credentials for profit.

Far more prevalent are everyday employees who inadvertently become part of the insider threat. People make mistakes configuring their environments. They may fail to prioritize patching. Budget cuts reduce investments in good security practices.

What happens is understandable. People want to get their jobs done faster and take shortcuts that unintentionally subvert security processes and tools. And sometimes people are simply tired from a night awake with a crying baby and accidentally click on a link in a phishing email that they wouldn't fall for on a good day.

This chapter explores how people can be a threat to or can help you protect your enterprise. First we'll look at the concerted threats from malicious outsiders. Then we will review the insider threat, with a goal of making everyone in your organization a part of the solution.

Cyberattacks: Who Is Behind External Threats?

Who are the attackers?

Threat actors may be hired by a nation-state, acting in an official government capacity. They may be activists committed to a cause. They may be part of a complex criminal enterprise, or they may simply be hackers for hire. Sometimes they play multiple roles: for example, a government employee may have a "side hustle" for profit.

In an attempt to attach threat actors to their TTPs (tactics, techniques, and procedures) and assign attribution, security companies come up with their own identifiers. The sometimes silly-sounding collection of proprietary names is dizzying. Just a quick lookup of the Fancy Bear group yields this Wikipedia description: "Fancy Bear[1] (also known as APT28 (by Mandiant[2]), Pawn Storm, Sofacy Group (by Kaspersky[3]), Sednit, Tsar Team (by FireEye[4]), and STRONTIUM (by Microsoft)[5]) is a Russian[6] cyber espionage[7] group."

You don't need to remember these funny names because those details aren't important for even the majority of people who work in cybersecurity.

What is far more important is that you take the time to find out what your organization has or does that might be of interest to a variety of types of threat actors and how you can help drive your organization toward greater security.

State-Sponsored Attacks

Nation-states are well-funded, sophisticated, and motivated by political, economic, and national security military reasons.

No one should be surprised that nations use cyberspace for espionage. After all, the world has moved online, so donning a disguise and photographing documents with a secret camera just doesn't make sense today. Modern nations have cyber intelligence-gathering programs. Israel and the US have some of the best programs—as do adversaries Russia, China, Iran, and North Korea.

Not surprisingly, attackers look for insiders to recruit. In 2015, a nation-state actor compromised the Office of Personnel Management[8] and security clearance contractors looking for government employees who may be good targets to compromise as espionage sources.

The recent SolarWinds[9] attacks show how Russia compromised the supply chain through a widely used IT vendor to gain access to information from government agencies and key companies. (Corrupted software updates seem to be a favorite technique for the Russians.)

SolarWinds also highlights an attack on a smaller vendor. While a larger firm like Microsoft or Amazon might have the resources to defend themselves, even those firms would probably struggle to fend off a targeted attack from a nation-state. It's worth considering that organizations would never be expected to defend themselves against physical attacks, but are somehow expected to fend off nation-state cyberattacks.

Nation-states also leverage cyber capabilities to degrade their adversaries' ability to respond in conflict—whether taking down a power facility or sabotaging other capabilities like nuclear centrifuges. Of course, nation-states use cyberspace for espionage; they are just updating espionage and combat techniques to the times.

But the goals of nation-state attacks have expanded from traditional national security intelligence and counterintelligence collection purposes, or even operational preparation of the environment for a time of conflict. We also see cases of personal revenge, such as the Iranian government's 2014 destructive malware attack on the Sands Casino[10]—because the CEO, Sheldon Adelson, insulted the Ayatollah. Another example is North Korea's attack on Sony based on the affront of the film *The Interview*. It is hard to fathom a country launching an attack in response to a Seth Rogen movie, but it happened.

Nation-states also use sophisticated online psychological operations to drive their national security goals, evidenced in Russian election interference using social media.[11]

Nations use cyberattacks for asymmetric projection of power, to show a nonmilitary "proportional response" to other nations. Sometimes the target for response is a private-sector company. For example, Iran launched distributed denial-of-service (DDoS) attacks against US financial institutions in retaliation for sanctions by the US government in 2012.[12]

Nation-states also leverage cyberattacks for economic advantage. China has stolen American trade secrets worth billions to help its economy leap forward and to give its own businesses an edge in negotiations and research and development. Why spend years working on a new formula when you can simply steal one from a US company? Why go into a contract negotiation cold when your government can get you the competition's proposal? Retired general Keith Alexander, former director of the NSA, has described it as the "greatest transfer of wealth in history."[13]

While the US government certainly does its fair share of spying for national security reasons, it does not spy to support American businesses. The Department of Homeland Security (DHS) has warned industry about Chinese intellectual property theft for years, and most recently warned about backdoors in Chinese products.

In a DHS press release, Acting Secretary Chad Wolfe pointed out that television manufacturer TCL receives support from the Chinese Communist Party to compete in the global electronics market. "TCL incorporated backdoors into all of its TV sets, exposing users to cyber breaches and data exfiltration," noted Wolfe.[14] Much more detail is available in the advisory document,[15] including concerns about "Made in China 2025," one of the Chinese government initiatives that share a goal of making that nation the leading global technological superpower by 2049.

This is nothing new; China has used these tactics for over a decade and simply continues to evolve and expand its TTPs.

Other nation-states seek financial benefit to fund their initiatives. Heavily sanctioned nations like North Korea have turned their army hackers to cybercrime to fill the regime's coffers. North Korea has leveraged attacks on crypto currency and financial institutions[16] to fund its weapons programs.

Cybercriminals

Cybercrime isn't about the stereotypical guy in his parents' basement; it is a sophisticated industry. In nations around the world with limited extradition potential and rule of law, criminals hack with impunity and have grown organizations that look like a large commercial company, with help desks, training, R&D departments, and money-back guarantees. Hacking provides economic opportunity in places where it is lacking. Like any successful business, practices and techniques evolved with the market landscape.[17]

When stolen credit card numbers and personal information flooded the dark web, driving down prices (supply and demand), cybercriminals ventured into malware as a service, business email compromise, sophisticated human-operated ransomware, and most recently DDoS for ransom.

Sometimes threat actors impersonate other known criminal groups.

Beginning in mid-2020, financial institutions began receiving letters sent to several organizations by actors posing as Fancy Bear or Lazarus Group.[18] No one actually believed these letters came from these nation-state actors, and few firms paid the ransom requested, but it shows the continuous evolution of criminal schemes.

Sometimes lines between nation-states and criminal actors blur. In late 2020, it was reported that threat actors behind Maze, Egregor, and Evil Corp are tied to the Russian government. Some reports claimed that Maze, Egregor, and Evil Corp are all one group operated by people within the Russian intelligence service. The US Treasury Department[19] had previously reported that Maksim Yakubets is involved in Evil Corp, and Mr. Yakubets is allegedly linked to the Russian government. Russia has also allegedly worked with criminal actors to leverage their tools and obfuscate attribution.

Government employees may also work for cybercrime organizations to supplement their income. At the end of the day, the organization ultimately directing these attacks matters less to businesses than the impact: ransomware attacks cost organizations $20 billion in 2020.[20]

As cybercriminals continue to evolve their tactics, they also grow the pool of cybercriminals. By selling malware as a service with training modules, they've lowered the barrier to entry to becoming a cybercriminal.

As criminals make more money, they invest in more advanced techniques, leveraging AI/ML (artificial intelligence/machine learning) and creating technology platforms for delivery.

Hacktivists

Hacktivists[21] are attackers who have a political or social agenda. They will damage or deface their targets to gain attention for a cause or shame a company or agency that they disagree with. They tend to be less skilled and sophisticated than nation-states and criminal groups. They may deface a less secure marketing website or steal and post poorly secured information about the company or its employees, even if the information isn't particularly sensitive. Anonymous is the best known hacktivist group, but others include the Syrian Electronic Army.

Key Tactics

Now that we have walked through the who and the why behind the attacks, we will talk a bit about how the attackers succeed.

Phishing

Social engineering continues to be the most common attack vector. Phishing is the fraudulent attempt to obtain personal information from individuals through emails purporting to be from reputable companies. Phishing remains king, from business email compromise to credential harvesting.

When phishing emails do not succeed, attackers send texts to get employees to click on a link or open a file to enable malware or, frequently in recent years, to steal credentials to access an organization's systems and data.

Phishers send messages that cast a wide net. They range from "Your email is over its size limit" to "Your bank account has been frozen" to "You have a package that can't be delivered." In the run-up to the 2020 holiday shopping season, the operators behind Dridex conducted a blast phishing scam that promised recipients a $100 Amazon gift card[22] but instead delivered a banking Trojan. The tactic was effective because in the time of COVID, most of us had packages on the way or something we planned to order from Amazon.

Phishing emails can also be far more sophisticated. Phishers target their prey based on their role in an organization, using LinkedIn and other sources to find a hook into an individual's interests and target those most likely to have access to the data and systems that the phishers want. They also target executives, in a practice known as "whaling," given the type of information they have access to and the likelihood they are less technically savvy.

A business email compromise (BEC) is a specific type of phishing attack that encourages employees to send money or data to a criminal posing as an executive or partner. Variations of the impersonation include the CEO asking Finance to wire money to a supplier right away, the CEO asking HR for all the W2s for the company, one firm asking another to change its wire transfer information, or a title company asking a property buyer to send a down payment. In some cases the threat actors have actually compromised the sender's email, but in many others an email is spoofed by making hard-to-spot changes in an email address (such as replacing the number 1 with a lowercase letter l) or saying the email is coming from a personal account.

Ransomware

Ransomware has dominated the cyberattack landscape for the past few years. Attacks on hospitals and first responders are particularly malicious, with the potential to impact patient health and safety. Of the more than 2,300 ransomware attacks in 2020 targeting educational, healthcare, and public sectors, 560 were aimed at the healthcare sector, according to Emsisoft's latest State of Ransomware[23] report.

Criminals no longer seek minor ransoms from small, less sophisticated victims. Now they are getting big money from household names and major cities. Ransoms started in hundreds to thousands and finally have reached up to the millions.

According to the Identity Theft Resource Center (ITRC), "The average ransomware payouts[24] for all businesses have grown from less than $10,000 in Q3 2018 to more than $178,000 per event by the end of Q2 2020. Large enterprises are making average ransomware payments of over $1 million." Ransomware has replaced large-scale data breaches as the criminal scheme of choice.

Threat actors—whether criminal or nation-state—are not only encrypting the data they ransom so their victims can't use it, but are also threatening to release stolen data publicly as another means to try to extort the money. This "name and shame" strategy has become pervasive.

This is just one way that ransomware actors have attempted to change the market dynamics. They realize that if there is confidence that paying a ransom will bring relief, they are more likely to get paid.

Breached companies now sometimes alert customers by sending letters that tell them not to worry, that the ransom was paid and their data is safe! This is a major change. Even the FBI has grown a bit more flexible about ransom payments,[25] acknowledging that sometimes organizations face complex decisions and urging victims to report incidents to the agency even if they choose to pay the ransom.

Ransomware exploits known vulnerabilities most of the time. While we have long talked about advanced persistent threats, "adequate persistent threats" continue to work as most attacks still leverage known, patchable vulnerabilities. But at the same time, as the threat actors make more money, they grow more sophisticated, mimicking the techniques of nation-state attackers.

As a result, human-operated ransomware attacks are more like advanced persistent threats. Once the ransomware is in a system connected to a network, it lurks, spreading laterally to other systems and escalating privileges while the criminal identifies the "crown jewels" of the victim, their most prized information resource. Attackers have been known to look for the victim's cyber insurance policy so they can set the ransom price based on deductibles and coverage. Because ransomware has spread across the network and attackers have done reconnaissance, when they are ready to strike, the attackers encrypt the network rapidly.[26]

The Insider Threat

In addition to a long list of outside actors, we are told we must beware the insider threat. But what does that really mean? We traditionally think of a disgruntled employee seeking revenge (think *Office Space*[27]) or an employee bribed for information. However, insiders can create a risk in a much broader way. Anybody with access to your systems or data—employees, former employees, partners, suppliers, contractors, and, thanks to the work-from-home boom, even family members and roommates—can open the door to an attack. Actions are not necessarily intentional and can occur because the insiders simply don't know any better. Despite best intentions, employees may accidentally give up credentials or click on files and links. Phishing can be very persuasive and targeted.

Accidental insiders are those employees who unwittingly cause harm or unauthorized access by doing things like clicking on malicious links, not following policies and procedures, or being careless.

One type of accidental insider is the employee who is legitimately trying to do their job but who doesn't want to be slowed down by complicated processes and technologies that impede their progress. They seek workarounds to meet their individual performance objectives by subverting security controls and in some cases creating a shadow IT environment.

Whether employees buy their own equipment or use a personal credit card to create cloud infrastructure, these rogue environments can compromise data, credentials, and broader environments. Cloud misconfigurations can easily happen in even the best of circumstances, as you may recall from the well-publicized Capital One breach.[28]

Despite the notoriety of that incident, more recently, a misconfigured cloud storage bucket exposed the personal details of hundreds of social media influencers.[29] An AWS S3 bucket misconfiguration at fashion social network 21 Buttons left data wide open with no encryption or password protection. Fifty million files were exposed, including invoices and payments, as well as personal information. The personally identifiable information (PII) exposed included full names, postal codes, bank details, national ID numbers, PayPal email addresses, and value of sales.

As companies focus on customer experience, security often takes a backseat to cool and efficient. There is constant tension in IT to meet business requirements and reduce risk. Security does not always win. In addition, cloud and SaaS solutions are rapidly evolving, and many people do not know how to configure them properly, inadvertently exposing data. There are simply not enough skilled personnel with knowledge of these tools and how to integrate them into a larger environment.

Sometimes overworked IT staff take shortcuts: not patching, allowing weak or default passwords, and so on. Again, employee experience and system performance sometimes takes priority over reducing security risk. With increased work from home, how many employees have kids using work computers for school and entertainment? How many employees have family members and roommates with access to corporate networks, either knowingly or unknowingly? How many overseas contractors had to switch to work from home? The attack surface and potential openings for attackers has grown with the critical need to maintain business operations in a rapidly changing environment. Security is part of a number of tradeoffs in a rapidly changing world.

Of course, security can also add cost that an organization may or may not be willing to pay. Over a decade ago, a colleague and I traveled on behalf of the Department of Homeland Security to an oil company in Houston. I sat in their office, stunned that they didn't feel concern or a sense of urgency when we—two senior leaders—traveled to their headquarters to tell them that a foreign government had infiltrated their network. They couldn't see why that was a problem warranting their activity or engagement; their defenses were poor. Their CIO and CISO hadn't invested in maintaining any logs, so forensics would have been difficult even if they had been interested. While not malicious, their decisions not to invest in security or even take a breach seriously made the IT and security leaders themselves a threat to their organization.

There are, of course, malicious insiders: employees with a deliberate intent to steal information or cause disruption. Usually these insiders seek financial gain, but they can also be disgruntled employees. This is why many companies carefully track employee activity and access when considering layoffs and even staff reductions due to COVID-19; desperate people can do desperate things. Other malicious insiders might be unhappy with their job, co-workers, pay, boss, or company direction. They can act independently or as an agent for another entity. Had this employee been less ethical or less loyal, he could have easily enabled a major breach.

In some cases, hospitals and health systems have been victims of malicious insiders who install Ryuk ransomware.[30] This targeted ransomware has led to an inability to access patient records, required the diversion of ambulances, and negatively impacted patient care. In Germany, ransomware is blamed for the death of a patient. Ryuk was used in the 2020 attack against Universal Health Services. "We're seeing a lot of insider threats,[31] unfortunately, where folks may recognize that their systems aren't patched as strongly as they should be or completely as they should be, and they're able to just insert this software right into some unsecured systems," said AMA Assistant Director of Federal Affairs Laura Hoffman.

Combating Insider Threats

What makes insider threats so hard to combat? Well, it's complicated.

Having a strong insider threat program requires walking a careful line with staff, unions, human resources, and legal counsel. You are dealing with people who others think they know and who have been trusted with the level of access needed to do their jobs.

Sometimes it is hard to decipher good and bad behavior, thus requiring sophisticated behavioral analytics. Security teams often lack the business context to understand what is expected, making those analytics hard. And of course it is sometimes harder to detect an insider from IT or security—they know what is being looked for and how to circumvent it. That is why regular review of privileged user behavior is so critical. Lack of tools, staff, policies, and processes make it very challenging to effectively manage the insider threat.

Simple best practices can certainly help prevent trouble. Limit access; only provide access to systems and data that people need to do their jobs, also known as "least privilege." And by their job, that means their current job, not the one they had five years ago. Regularly review access entitlements. Create a separation of duties to provide checks and balances, and require dual authorization for sensitive activities, whether sending large wire transfers or maintaining crypto keys.

What should your insider threat program be looking for? Security teams should look for the following behaviors, whether purposely malicious or simply egregious policy violations that expose the company to risk:

- Unauthorized use of IT resources and applications
- Employees using unauthorized cloud accounts for storage of corporate information
- Rogue use of shadow IT
- Accessing, sharing, or distributing personally identifiable information
- Installing unapproved and unlicensed software
- Unauthorized use of restricted applications, including network sniffing and remote desktop tools
- Unauthorized transfer of data or using removable media to store or move data
- Unauthorized copying of business-critical data to a cloud or web service
- Transferring files to and from unusual destinations
- Moving files using instant messenger or social media applications
- Misuse, abuse, and malicious behavior
- Misusing file system administrator rights
- Disabling or overriding endpoint security products
- Using password cracking tools such as John the Ripper and Hashcat
- Accessing the dark web or nonwork-related sites

What can you do to minimize unintentional insider threats and help make all employees part of the solution? Create a robust and continuous security awareness training program that includes education and training, not just for new employees or once a year, but on an ongoing basis. Everyone has to be part of the team.

Phishing testing is a valuable part of such a program and should present increasing difficulty and change with the time of year and roles of employees. For example, in February test employees with Secret Admirer emails or send messages about a new benefit package that seem to come from HR. Customize phishing test messages to the business context of particular departments. For example, you might send general counsel employees information about free continuing legal education courses or send the accounting department fake business email compromise lures based on the latest real-world attack messages.

Employees should know to report something that looks out of the norm and know whom they should report it to. One employee may be on the ball and spot a phish; another may be moving fast, or on a mobile device, and miss it. Reporting should always be encouraged, and possibly reinforced with a badge or thank-you email. In working with developers, explain why security is so important, even if it causes friction. Gain buy-in and build knowledge for shared responsibility through a security champion program with your development teams. Security built in from the start is always preferable to, and cheaper than, after the fact.

Again, creating these messages requires circumspection. HR, Legal, and Corporate Communications have roles to play in defining how insider threats are handled. Security teams must make sure they don't create a culture where employees feel mistrust because in most cases employees have good intentions.

Ask business owners to provide you with context so you can tell a relevant, compelling story without security jargon. What would happen to your customers and your business if confidentiality, integrity, or availability were impacted by a cyberattack? People can become numb to news reports of cyber incidents; it is important to make the risk real for them. People want to feel part of the team and appreciated. They want to be seen as valued contributors and often feel connected to customers and to the corporate mission.

Is it true that people can be your first line of defense, or should they be your last line of defense? Should we expect technology to stop everything? While the latest security tools and platforms move us closer to end-to-end security, as discussed in Chapter 14, employees should also feel that they are an important part of the security team. Adversaries are smart and constantly evolving, and we need everyone on the alert.

We need to train our employees to be suspicious if something feels odd or seems not quite right, reinforcing the adage, "If you see something, say something." It might be an email from the CEO's personal account asking for a financial transfer, a call from IT asking for password information, a strange pop-up asking for credentials, or a stranger wandering around the office. Encourage people to ask questions rather than being afraid to slow down a process or appear unhelpful or paranoid.

Employees regularly catch phishing emails not caught by sophisticated systems. Employees notice strange system behavior or inquiries received that just seem outside the norm. They know their jobs, processes, and applications better than a centralized cybersecurity team and should be brought into the conversation about the threat landscape and what bad actors might exploit in their unique work environment.

Employees can also help you understand the crown jewels that an adversary might be interested in. A friend at the CIA used to say, "If you're interested in China, China is interested in you." How will the security team know about a plan to enter into a joint venture or bid on a new contract related to China if there isn't a partnership with the business? Consider creating a business information security officer program to strengthen that link and to help ensure security is built into new systems and processes and that there is a link with security to help the business understand emerging threats and evolving risks.

Conclusion

By the time this book is published, the cyber threat landscape will no doubt have changed and evolved. There will be new variants of malware, new schemes and scams, and new catchy names for actor groups. Geopolitics will cause nation-states to target one another as interests shift.

But what has stayed the same? The bad guys will continue to use our new tools and technologies to steal what they need and drive their objectives. The rewards of cyberattacks will cause our adversaries to innovate and improve their TTPs as we advance our defenses. At the same time, most intrusions will result from our employees falling for a phish and a failure to prioritize patching.

We simply are not forcing people to bring their A game. If a nation-state like Russia truly wants to access your specific corporate network, you likely cannot stop them with even the best and most expensive commercial cybersecurity program. But you can make yourself a more challenging target for other attackers, not falling prey to the latest attacker "blast" campaign.

Stay up to speed, continue to talk about risk with your business partners and employees, and make the investments needed to ensure that you aren't the example cited in the next edition of this book.

Notes

1.   https://en.wikipedia.org/wiki/Fancy_Bear
2.   https://en.wikipedia.org/wiki/Mandiant
3.   https://en.wikipedia.org/wiki/Kaspersky_Lab

4. https://en.wikipedia.org/wiki/FireEye

5. https://en.wikipedia.org/wiki/Microsoft

6. https://en.wikipedia.org/wiki/Russia

7. https://en.wikipedia.org/wiki/Cyber_spying

8. https://fas.org/sgp/crs/natsec/R44111.pdf

9. https://cyber.dhs.gov/ed/21-01/

10. https://thehill.com/policy/cybersecurity/226915-iranian-hackers-downed-us-casino-empire

11. https://www.brennancenter.org/our-work/analysis-opinion/new-evidence-shows-how-russias-election-interference-has-gotten-more

12. https://www.justice.gov/opa/pr/seven-iranians-working-islamic-revolutionary-guard-corps-affiliated-entities-charged

13. https://www.foxbusiness.com/politics/chinese-theft-of-us-intellectual-property-greatest-transfer-of-wealth-in-history

14. https://www.dhs.gov/news/2020/12/21/acting-secretary-chad-f-wolf-remarks-prepared-homeland-security-and-china-challenge

15. https://www.dhs.gov/publication/data-security-business-advisory

16. https://www.reuters.com/article/us-northkorea-cyber-un-idUSKCN1UV1ZX

17. https://www.zdnet.com/article/cybercrime-and-cyberwar-a-spotters-guide-to-the-groups-that-are-out-to-get-you/

18. https://www.radware.com/security/ddos-threats-attacks/threat-advisories-attack-reports/global-ransom-ddos-campaign-update/

19. https://home.treasury.gov/news/press-releases/sm845

20. https://threatpost.com/ransomware-2020-extortion/162319/

21. https://corporatefinanceinstitute.com/resources/knowledge/other/hacktivism/

22. https://www.darkreading.com/threat-intelligence/amazon-gift-card-scam-delivers-dridex-this-holiday-season/d/d-id/1339810

23. https://blog.emsisoft.com/en/37314/the-state-of-ransomware-in-the-us-report-and-statistics-2020/

24. https://www.infosecurity-magazine.com/news/criminals-favor-ransomware-bec/

25. https://www.ic3.gov/Content/PDF/Ransomware_Fact_Sheet.pdf

26. https://www.zdnet.com/article/ransomware-gangs-are-getting-faster-at-encrypting-networks-that-will-make-them-harder-to-stop/

27. https://www.imdb.com/title/tt0151804/

28. https://www.capitalone.com/digital/facts2019/

29. https://www.infosecurity-magazine.com/news/misconfigured-bucket-exposes/

30. https://us-cert.cisa.gov/ncas/alerts/aa20-302a

31. https://www.korchek.com/blog/beware-of-insider-cyber-threats-ama-warns-hospitals/

JENNY MENNA

Jenny Menna has executive security experience in government, financial services, and most recently the healthcare industry. Her current and past industry leadership roles include the FS-ISAC Board of Directors, the Global Cybersecurity Alliance Strategic Advisory Committee, the Financial Top Level Domain Board of Directors, the Risk Committee of Early Warning Services, and the National Cybersecurity Alliance Board of Directors. She is a Visiting Fellow at George Mason University's National Security Institute.

Prior to transitioning to lead business security risk for a major healthcare company, she served as the Deputy CISO for US Bank. Jenny also held a variety of senior cybersecurity leadership positions in the Department of Homeland Security. Her responsibilities ranged from industry outreach to frontline operational and technical activities—from serving as US-CERT Director to leading national-level policy initiatives. She received awards for her work under both the Bush and Obama Administrations, and the inaugural Excellence Award from the Multi-State Information Sharing and Analysis Center for her leadership in advancing state and local government cybersecurity. She was selected for the Senior Executive Service in 2009. Jenny received both her bachelor's and master's degrees from the University of Chicago. Jenny is a Certified Information Security Manager.

5 | Addressing the Skills and Diversity Gap

LISA DONNAN

W ITH MILLIONS MORE JOBS THAN WORKERS, THE DEMAND for both frontline cybersecurity workers and leaders is outpacing the supply. Beyond the overall shortage of cybersecurity workers, a vast diversity gap encompasses every facet of diversity, including race, ethnicity, orientation, and disability status. Most notably females, who make up half the population, comprise only about 24% of cybersecurity workers.[1]

This chapter offers guidance to CISOs on ways to bridge the skills and diversity gap as well as advice to anyone seeking a job in cybersecurity. Moreover, without inclusion as part of the equation, bridging the gap will not be as successful or long-term. It is like recruiting for a sports team: one part of the task is hiring the diversity, and the other is putting that talent on the field. If you hire diverse candidates and then keep them on the bench, you have not moved the ball—or the strategy—forward.

Assessing the Skills Gap

The need for cybersecurity workers is immense.[2] Cybersecurity Ventures[3] estimates the shortage at 3.5 million and notes that every IT position is a cybersecurity position now.

A majority of CISOs[4] are worried about the skills gap. Fortinet research[5] found that more than two-thirds of organizations struggle to recruit, hire, and retain cybersecurity talent. That struggle translates into real problems. Nearly three-fourths of organizations experienced a breach or intrusion within the last year that can be at least partially attributed to a shortage of cybersecurity workers within the organization. Nearly half saw three or more such breaches.

To meet the projected demand, the cybersecurity workforce needs to grow by 145% globally and 62% in the United States.

If you're a CISO, that gap represents an alarming, compelling trend. If you're interested in working in cybersecurity, that gap presents an excellent career opportunity.

Assessing the Diversity Gap

From the front lines to the CISO, women are underrepresented and underpaid in cybersecurity. Although females represent just over half of the population, they comprise a little less than a quarter of security professionals.[6] About 15% of organizations have no women working in cybersecurity at all.

There are plenty of contributing factors for this glass ceiling, including a lack of female mentors, female role models, and work environments that do not support or retain women. In fact, 22% of women reported experiencing discrimination at work, compared to 13% of men.[7] Women in STEM jobs such as cybersecurity face several kinds of gender bias at work, including pressure to prove themselves over and over, competition for the token female spot on a team, having to walk a tightrope between being seen as too feminine to be competent and too masculine to be likable, and, finally, isolation. Women in cyber are also paid an average of 21% less than men.

Research[8] by HP and HBR shows that in general women are less likely than men to apply for jobs if they don't think that they have all the qualifications listed. This trend applies right up to the CISO; Fortinet research[9] found that a mere 7% of CISO résumés come from women.

The scarcity of female leaders in cybersecurity exacerbates the gender gap because female role models, when they exist, both inspire women to enter the field and help women move ahead.

As for minorities (defined by the US Census Bureau as Black, American Indian, Asian, Pacific Islander, Hispanic, or two or more races), they are making inroads, but results are mixed, according to (ISC)[2]'s Innovation Through Inclusion.[10] The good news: minorities hold 26% of cybersecurity jobs, roughly in line with their 28% representation in the US population.

The bad news:

- Minorities are less likely to be in cybersecurity leadership positions. Only 23% of minority cybersecurity professionals hold a role of director or above, compared to 30% of their Caucasian peers.

- Minorities earned less: $115,000 compared to the overall US cybersecurity workforce average of $122,000. Men of color in cybersecurity earn $3,000 less than white men.

- Women of color fared the worst; they earn an average of $10,000 less than white men and $6,000 less than white women.

- Compared to other races and ethnicities, Caucasian workers were more likely to have received a raise within the last year.

- Nearly one-third (32%) of minority cybersecurity professionals reported they had experienced discrimination at work.

The Power of Diverse Teams

Hiring and promoting diversity isn't just the right thing to do; diverse teams drive business success. For example, increases in racial diversity were clearly related to enhanced financial performance for innovation-focused banks (Scientific American[11]). More broadly, McKinsey[12] found that companies in the top quartile for gender or racial and ethnic diversity are more likely to achieve financial returns above national industry medians.

Focusing on the gender gap, a global survey[13] of 22,000 firms found that companies that went from no female corporate leaders to a 30% female share saw a 1% increase in net margin, which translates to a 15% increase in profitability for a typical firm. The increased gender diversity powered success by increasing skill diversity in upper management and by lowering gender discrimination throughout the company, which helped firms recruit top talent.

Addressing the gender gap in cybersecurity alone would have an important impact on the US economy. Closing cybersecurity's gender gap would boost the US economy by $30 billion, with an additional $12.7 billion if women earned as much as their male colleagues (Forbes Technology Council).[14]

The improved financial performance makes sense because increased diversity of cybersecurity talent equals diverse ways to solve problems. Female CISOs scored higher than their male counterparts in both leadership (46%) and analytical skills (150%), according to analysis from Fortinet.[15]

Diverse teams enable innovation and creativity. Not only do people with diverse backgrounds bring new information and perspectives, but simply having diverse teams in an organization forces other workers to prepare better, to be open to alternate viewpoints, and to strive harder to reach consensus.

Of course, correlation does not equal causation; greater diversity in corporate leadership doesn't automatically translate into more profit, according to McKinsey (cited earlier). But the correlation does indicate that when companies commit themselves to diverse leadership, they become more successful.

Bridging the Skills and Diversity Gaps

Actively working to bridge the diversity gap also helps bridge the skills gap because in so doing your organization opens the doors to additional cybersecurity workers—women and underrepresented people of color—you may not have considered before. Instead of hiring for cultural fit, CISOs and those hiring in cybersecurity should be more open to candidates who don't look like them, who have different experiences and different backgrounds, and who are outside their circle of friends and colleagues.

Speaking of opening doors, open houses and job fairs are effective ways to get good candidates of all varieties into your organization. As you sift through candidates, tweak your résumé-evaluating algorithms to allow consideration of applicants who do not necessarily check every box on your qualifications list. The added value and contributions these diverse candidates bring can make up the difference in missing skills. Then, your organization can support these new employees in earning any needed certifications and training to close their personal skills gaps.

Military veterans and their spouses represent another pool of skilled workers who are poised to bridge the skills gap. Many veterans are highly trained in technology. When asked about their veteran colleagues, more than 40% of respondents to the Fortinet skills shortage survey cited their work ethic, their attention to detail, and their ability to work in fast-paced, high-stress environments. Respondents also praised veterans' decision-making abilities, discipline, and can-do attitude. Ideally, those values will spill over into your entire corporate culture.

While new hires are important, not all of your cybersecurity workers have to come from outside your organization. One way to increase your supply is to recruit from within. Leveraging existing staff to make lateral moves to join your security team and building on their existing skills and expertise could provide another avenue to hiring. This is an excellent way to grow those employees' skill sets while producing cross- and multi-disciplinary teams and creating greater collaboration. All cybersecurity workers do not need to be technology-based experts. Human resources, marketing, communications, and other functional workers may have the ability to contribute by building on their existing skill sets.

Once cybersecurity professionals are on the job, you want them to stay. But many of your fellow cybersecurity leaders as well as the workers on their teams are keeping one eye on the exit. More than half of CISOs said senior security leaders remain in their jobs for an average of less than three years.[16] Frontline cybersecurity workers are also under pressure; the Ponemon Institute[17] reports that about two-thirds (65%) have considered quitting because of high stress levels. About three-fourths (77%) get a call from recruiters to see if they are ready to change jobs at least once a month.

Improving corporate culture, both overall and specifically for a diverse workforce, is critical. The skills gap is a major part of the problem. Overall, cybersecurity workers feel overworked. Two-thirds of respondents working in organizations that have been impacted by the skills gap say that the shortage of cybersecurity workers has resulted in increased workload on the existing staff, according to a 2019 ISSA/ESG survey.[18] Nearly half (47%) said they don't have enough time to fully learn and utilize the security technologies they already have.

To retain talent, it's critical to cultivate a culture of inclusiveness where candidates from diverse backgrounds can not only survive, but thrive. That culture isn't always present today. As stated earlier, both women and underrepresented people of color report bias and discrimination in technology jobs. A culture of inclusion produces numerous benefits across the organization, including positive impacts on employee roles in cybersecurity retention, engagement, and financial performance.

Status, perception, and company politics are also important. Corporate leaders often see cybersecurity as a cost center, comparable to the after-hours cleaning service, because it doesn't bring in revenue. That approach is short-sighted and is rapidly evolving, thanks to the pressure boards of directors are putting on companies' cybersecurity programs. The rise in litigation against CEOs and boards of directors regarding data breaches and failure to implement risk management plans has resulted in a media frenzy. Moreover, in 2018 the Securities and Exchange Commission provided guidance with strong views regarding the board's essential role in the statement "cybersecurity risks should be disclosed if cybersecurity risks are material to a company's business."

Such disclosures should address how a board "engages with management on cybersecurity issues" and "discharges its cybersecurity risk oversight."

Consequently, even though cybersecurity doesn't bring in revenue, a good cybersecurity program saves money: the average cost of a data breach[20] in 2020 was $3.86 million. The savings from preventing just one data breach could pay for a team of cybersecurity workers. In general, perceptions need to change to considering cybersecurity as essential to the business, not as cyber janitors. Increasing the visibility and respect for the CISO will help not just the CISO but also frontline workers who report to the CISO. Furthermore, cybersecurity has matured, gaining authority to speak to the CEO and the board.

Additionally, increasing pay is an important way to attract new talent and retain the people you already have. In 2016 the federal government[21] began offering extra pay to attract and retain talented cybersecurity workers. Improving workplace pay and culture will improve morale, attract new talent, help you retain the talent you have, and spread the workload around, thus reducing stress levels.

Building out your five- to fifteen-year pipeline of workers is similarly important. Encourage your company to sponsor hackathons, coding contests, school visits, and other programs for middle and high school students, especially girls and underrepresented people of color, to encourage interest from students.

For high school and college students, your organization can sponsor shadowing opportunities, apprenticeships, and internships to attract your cybersecurity team members over the next five years and possibly your CISO ten years down the line.

Advice for Those Starting a Career in Cybersecurity

Today's careers require us to reinvent ourselves multiple times. You can start a career in cybersecurity at any stage in your professional life. Think outside the box; you don't need a four-year degree in computer science to work in cyber. No matter what your background is—English, history, or other liberal arts—there is a security career for you. The only question is where to start. Potential jobs include security analyst and penetration tester, as well as roles in risk and compliance, privacy, sales, marketing, product development, and quality assurance.

If you don't know what specific area you're interested in, start looking from a broader perspective. As discussed earlier, consider adjacency and lateral moves. In whatever role or field you're already in, start working on its cybersecurity aspects. Then, look into acquiring additional skills and moving deeper into the areas of cybersecurity that interest you most.

Certifications are often a path to a security career. More than 80% of those responding to the Fortinet survey on the skills shortage[22] have earned certificates themselves, and 85% say someone on their team has earned a certification. Ninety-four percent of those who have earned certifications believe the additional education has better prepared them for their current role. Some 82% of employers prefer to hire someone who has earned a certification. Some certifications to consider include Certified Information System Security Professional (CISSP), Certified Information Security Manager (CISM), Certified Information Systems Auditor (CISA), and Certified Cloud Security Professional (CCSP).

Some courses are inexpensive, and others are even free. For example, Udacity.com offers a free course in network security[23] through Georgia Tech (see the appendix for additional training resources). Finally, explore options including in-house security training, webinars, and online courses. Pay particular attention to local networking opportunities, including security meetups.[24]

To Move Up, Think Outside the Box

Employers are looking for CISO candidates with soft skills in leadership, communications, planning, risk management, and operational skills. They are looking for hard skills in compliance, incident and response management, data protection, and how to quickly minimize the impact of a breach and quickly remediate the issue. As stated earlier, women have an inherent advantage in leadership and analytical skills but a reluctance to apply when they fear they're not fully qualified. When you apply for a job, know what you're bringing to the table.

Opportunities definitely exist for women and other diverse candidates willing to step out and ask, even if you aren't yet fully qualified. To diversify their teams, companies experiencing security challenges may be willing to take a chance on a candidate who doesn't have all the required skills. In the meantime, traditional candidates may not want to take a chance on companies experiencing problems, opening another door for members of underrepresented groups. Industries that are growing also are more likely to give underrepresented candidates a chance. It is important to remember that even if you aren't fully qualified on paper, you should be willing to pursue it.

As noted earlier, education is one key to moving up. As you aspire to a CISO job, a master's or bachelor's degree in information technology, with a focus on cybersecurity, is one path to gain leadership and IT skills. If you aspire to the CISO role, another pathway is to earn an MBA so you can better communicate with business leaders and the board. You can find additional resources in the appendix.

If you aspire to use a CISO job to move up even higher in your company or another company, evolution within the industry is opening those doors. As the CISO role gains visibility, more CISOs are now reporting directly to the corporate general counsel, to the board, or directly to the CEO. As CISOs attain wider recognition and the role becomes increasingly important, high performers are positioned to move even higher. Key skill sets for those roles will be financial and operational metrics.

Conclusion

We can make progress in filling the skills gap as we address the diversity gap. Women and members of other underrepresented diverse groups make up significant untapped potential to meet needs in cybersecurity. We need to be open to what they bring to the table and be willing to pay for and foster education to add new skills. To attract skilled talent across all groups, we need to build cultures of retention and inclusiveness with a team focus on success where people feel supported and have the resources to do their jobs. Closing the diversity gap also will bring about a fundamental shift in addressing our approach to security across organizations of all sizes, public and private.

While the actions recommended in this chapter move us in the right direction, it must be said that they do not address a fundamental issue in the educational system in the United States, which is the lack of female engineering students. To encourage more women to go into this field, we have to rethink our educational system much further back in the pipeline. The cybersecurity skills and diversity gaps are best served in a world where young girls are educated in a way that opens the door to engineering programs. This is not true today, and without deliberate effort, we have little hope of closing the gender gap long-term.

We must all work toward building an inclusive culture that encourages both girls and boys to participate in coding and robotics camps and competitions. Corporate partnerships, sponsorships, employee volunteer programs, and mentoring programs are among the ways that we can encourage long-term change that will address critical gaps in both skills and diversity.

Notes

1. https://www.isc2.org/research/women-in-cybersecurity

2. https://www.isc2.org/Research/-/media/6573BE9062B64FC7B4B91F20ECC56299.ashx

3. https://cybersecurityventures.com/jobs/

4. https://hbr.org/sponsored/2019/06/the-public-private-partnership-thats-working-to-make-new-york-city-a-global-hub-of-cybersecurity-talent

5. https://www.fortinet.com/content/dam/maindam/PUBLIC/02_MARKETING/08_Report/report-fortinet-survey-skills-shortage.pdf

6. https://www.isc2.org/research/women-in-cybersecurity

7. https://www.infosecurity-magazine.com/news/women-in-cybersecurity-paid-21/

8. https://hbr.org/2014/08/why-women-dont-apply-for-jobs-unless-theyre-100-qualified

9. https://www.fortinet.com/resources-campaign/ciso/the-ciso-ascends-from-technologist-to-strategic-business-enabler-2

10. https://www.isc2.org/-/media/Files/Research/Innovation-Through-Inclusion-Report.ashx

11. https://www.scientificamerican.com/article/how-diversity-makes-us-smarter/

12. https://www.mckinsey.com/featured-insights/diversity-and-inclusion/diversity-wins-how-inclusion-matters

13. https://www.piie.com/system/files/documents/wp16-3.pdf

14. https://www.forbes.com/sites/forbestechcouncil/2020/05/20/closing-cybersecuritys-gender-gap-can-aid-the-skills-shortage-and-the-economy/?sh=21fefde3495a

15. https://www.fortinet.com/resources-campaign/ciso/the-ciso-ascends-from-technologist-to-strategic-business-enabler-2

16. https://media.nominet.uk/wp-content/uploads/2019/02/12130924/Nominet-Cyber_CISO-report_FINAL-130219.pdf

17. https://www.devo.com/resources/ponemon-soc-effectiveness-report-2019/

18. https://www.globenewswire.com/news-release/2019/05/09/1821287/0/en/Cybersecurity-Skills-Shortage-Worsening-for-Third-Year-In-A-Row-Sounding-the-Alarm-for-Business-Leaders.html

19. https://corpgov.law.harvard.edu/2018/03/13/sec-guidance-on-public-company-cybersecurity-disclosures/

20. https://www.ibm.com/security/data-breach

21. https://www.opm.gov/policy-data-oversight/pay-leave/reference-materials/handbooks/compensation-flexibilities-to-recruit-and-retain-cybersecurity-professionals.pdf

22. https://www.fortinet.com/content/dam/maindam/PUBLIC/02_MARKETING/08_Report/report-fortinet-survey-skills-shortage.pdf

23. https://www.udacity.com/course/network-security--ud199

24. https://www.meetup.com/ is one source for local in-person events.

LISA DONNAN

In the wake of cyber warfare, Lisa Donnan is at the forefront of successfully commercializing innovative and disruptive technologies, launching new businesses and markets in the public and private sectors. Lisa is a world-class operating executive with over 25 years of expertise in national security and commercial markets. She is a recognized thought leader in cybersecurity, artificial intelligence, and social media data analytics.

Lisa currently is a Partner at Option3Ventures, LLC, a private equity specialist firm that focuses solely on cybersecurity. Lisa serves as Chairman on the Volgenau College of Engineering Board of Directors and as Chairman of Federal Relations at George Mason University. She also serves on the National Defense Industrial Association Board of Directors.

PART TWO
Process

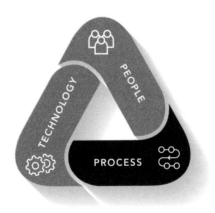

C YBERSECURITY IS NO LONGER ONLY THE DOMAIN OF YOUR IT and security teams. From the loading dock to the C-suite, everyone must be security minded.

The connection between your people and the security technology you invest in is encapsulated in processes.

Processes Bridge How People Use Technology

Sound processes build a bridge between your people and your technology. With the right processes in place, articulated in clear policies, people know up front what they should and should not do. Sound cybersecurity processes and policies limit employee access to only the data they need to do their jobs, and the right processes can ensure that employees protect and properly use the data your people do need.

To be mature, processes need to be clearly defined, agile, easy to follow, measurable, and repeatable. Written policies should be clear and succinct to ensure that everyone understands what they should do.

Defining processes and putting them in place is not a one-time effort. Maintaining cybersecurity is a continuous, evolving process. On a regular basis, you need to review your policies and processes to determine if they're still effective or if they need to be modified.

This section covers process areas of urgent concern for CISOs, including cyber risk management, blending NOC and SOC, secure development, compliance, and supply chain risk.

Cyber Risk Management

Cyber risk management entails assessing all of your risks from a cybersecurity perspective and deciding how to measure, manage, and communicate those risks.

Risk management is familiar territory for business leaders, but cyber risk management requires additional expertise and understanding. Security leaders recognize that cyber risk cannot be reduced to zero; some security incidents are inevitable.

Cyber risks must be evaluated within the larger context of business strategy and goals. Every organization has to define its risk appetite, deciding how much risk is acceptable.

Cyber risk management is an area where CISOs have an opportunity to show their business leadership. Participating in relevant committees and working groups in areas such as data privacy and risk is one important way to ensure that cyber risks are brought to light and communicated clearly. Metrics should be developed that offer rapid insight into whether cyber risk is within the stated risk tolerance.

Overall, you want to build a technology portfolio that mitigates cyber risk as much as possible given budget constraints. Since you cannot eliminate all risk, you have to be transparent about potential risk. The security team should make sure other teams acknowledge and accept the potential vulnerabilities associated with new software and technology that they adopt.

Chapter 6 describes your strategic role in cyber risk management.

Blending NOC And SOC

Traditionally, the Network Operations Center and the Security Operations Center operated as silos, with the NOC handling hardware failures and network errors and the SOC defending against hackers. That approach doesn't work in today's environment.

Because of the way today's attacks are happening, you don't necessarily know whether a problem has been caused by a hard drive going bad or an attack by an adversary. When an incident happens, your only saving grace is how quickly you respond. The goal is to improve your threat intelligence by getting your cyber response to network speeds. By blending NOC and SOC operations, we can better achieve that goal.

While the exact methodology for blending NOC and SOC varies by organization, in all cases, people in charge of those areas need clear processes and checklists in place, as well as an opportunity to exercise those processes together.

Chapter 7 covers practical issues related to blending NOC and SOC operations.

Secure Application Development

Security should not be an afterthought, especially when it comes to writing code. Yet many organizations struggle to incorporate security as a metric for code quality.

Secure application development means being proactive and training your developers in secure coding practices and empowering them to become security champions. To achieve this goal, you need processes in place that ensure regular training sessions for development teams. In addition, secure development and security awareness training should be part of onboarding, required before newly hired developers put their hands on keyboards.

Organizations need resources and processes in place so that developers and architects have access to security engineers as questions arise and when designing new features.

Secure development entails knowing what libraries are in use and ensuring they are patched and up to date. Secure development means being vigilant about vulnerabilities in the technology stack and ensuring that patches and updates are applied in a timely manner.

Organizational processes need to change to prioritize secure development. The overall development and release schedule must include tasks that ensure security, building in time for patching, fixes, and code review. Customers expect secure code, and you need processes in place to make this an integral part of product management.

Chapter 8 offers strategies for creating an effective secure development program.

Compliance

From a compliance standpoint, organizations must navigate an alphabet soup of evolving privacy and security regulations and standards. Privacy has been brought to the forefront by regulations like the EU's GDPR and California's CCPA. The panoply of regulations faced by any given organization depends in part on the industry, some of which are highly regulated. For example, healthcare organizations are subject to HIPAA, while any organization that processes credit or bank card transactions must implement PCI-DSS.

For security, organizations may choose to adopt frameworks from NIST, ISO, or others. Ultimately, you need a framework against which to measure and strengthen your organization's security posture. Frameworks provide a road map for benchmarking your security controls.

Chapter 9 covers the ins and outs of compliance processes and how to collaborate with the rest of the organization in this key area.

Supply Chain Risk

Beyond your own organization and employees, you need processes that protect your entire enterprise from end to end, which includes your supply chain. After all, a risk assumed by one is a risk assumed by all. Organizations are often impacted by actions across several levels of their supply chains.

In the past, organizations selected a vendor for a service or a product—whether new software, a marketing tool, an HVAC system, or a custodial service. Then, they simply brought the product or service into their network, often without analyzing the potential risks. From a security standpoint, that approach is a nonstarter. If you're using SaaS, it is run by another company. If that software is not secured properly, you're putting your organization at risk. If a third-party software, service, or product has a vulnerability, you've just added an unforeseen—and harder to locate—vulnerability to your own network. For example, the 2013 Target hack[1] started with stolen credentials from a third-party vendor, an HVAC company.

A breach at any point in your supply chain can compromise your security. Security leaders must make prudent decisions that reflect this reality. Vetting potential vendors and supply chain partners for security weaknesses and other problems is critical. You must also be aware of the risks of single points of failure along your supply chain. Bottom line: you need to understand and properly vet your entire supply chain.

Chapter 10 covers supply chain risk.

Security is not an absolute, because no one has unlimited money or unlimited resources to invest. Given that you cannot reduce risk to zero, the best guidance for establishing effective processes requires gauging your organization's risk tolerance, as described next.

Note

1. https://krebsonsecurity.com/2014/02/target-hackers-broke-in-via-hvac-company/

Effective Cyber Risk Management Requires Broad Collaboration

SUZANNE HARTIN AND MARIA S. THOMPSON

WHY DOES CYBER RISK MANAGEMENT DESERVE A CHAPTER in this book? Isn't that what we've been doing all along? Managing our cyber risk? Well, yes and no.

Given the world we've lived in, our focus has been on the right things—patching, managing incidents, ensuring we have the right firewall rules, securing our data in the cloud, and so on. But in today's world, with the CISO required to be a strategist and business promoter, considerations and requirements have grown much more expansive and include questions like:

- Are we managing our cyber risk to fall within our company's cyber risk appetite?
- Are we sufficiently considering other risks interwoven with cybersecurity?
- How do changes in the external environment, such as the plethora of new privacy regulations, impact our security programs?
- Are we even sure we're considering all the risks we should?

Answering these questions accurately is vital since the success of the cybersecurity program is critical to achieving corporate objectives.

Understanding Your Organization's Risk Appetite

First, let's look at identifying the level of risk your organization is willing to take, its risk appetite. The ISO 31000 risk management standard defines risk appetite as "the amount and type of risk that an organization is prepared to pursue, retain, or take."

We all have a personal risk appetite even though we may not explicitly acknowledge it. Here are some indications of personal risk appetite:

- We buy insurance or we don't.
- We exceed the speed limit or we don't.
- We try extreme sports or we don't.

The same is true of companies, many of which have begun to document their risk appetite in a risk appetite statement and measure performance against it. Risk appetite is generally specified in the context of a company's strategic objectives.

Understanding your business is key to composing a risk appetite statement. Consider whether your organization is public or private, single-threaded or running a multitude of differing business lines, consumer facing or business-to-business. These factors all inform the risk appetite of the organization, which is then captured in one or more risk appetite statements.

The complexity of the organization will dictate whether there is one overall risk appetite statement or one for each department or business unit. For example, in a large public organization, you may have various entities that deal with highly sensitive data, requiring stringent privacy and security measures such as citizen taxes, safety services, or critical infrastructure along with other entities that support museums and other recreational facilities. While these entities all form a single citizen-facing unit, it would be difficult to argue that they all share the same risk appetite.

Let's look at some simple examples. A broad operational risk appetite statement is "We will control our operational activities and exposure to avoid an event resulting in a loss to pre-tax operating margin of more than $20 million." A more specific example is "We will control fraud losses to within 10 basis points" or, in the case of a recreational facility, "We will control activities in such a way as to ensure fewer than four visitor injuries of any kind per year."

These examples raise two questions: What happens when you don't have an easy metric, such as dollars, against which to craft your risk appetite statement? And what happens if you temporarily exceed your appetite for risk? Exceeding your threshold is okay if you have established a "risk tolerance" level that the company has agreed is temporarily acceptable. However, taking the steps required to get back within the appetite is mandatory at that point.

As to the first question, it's often the case in information security that we don't have easily calculated, specific metrics to answer the question "Are we operating within our organization's cyber risk appetite?" Therefore, most companies wind up with a general statement as to their appetite for cyber risk with a limit of "low" or "medium." The catch is then twofold: If the defined risk limit is "low," is that really feasible in today's world? And second, how can you know with certainty that you're within your risk appetite without a hard number to measure against?

Measuring Actual Risk Against Risk Appetite

We all know that we can't answer the question "Are we secure?" with any certitude because even if we're actually secure at this precise moment, we might not be in the next hour, given all the changes in our business environments, in our hardware, in our software, and in the world outside our virtual walls. But organizations must constantly figure out if they're secure enough.

Key components of understanding whether security is adequate include whether the organization is detecting what they should, preventing what they should, remediating issues rapidly enough, and keeping up with all the ever-changing factors that impact our security.

Crafting a set of metrics, or key risk indicators (KRIs), for the information security program to address each of these areas is critical for understanding variance between actual performance and risk appetite targets. Each KRI needs to have a threshold that aligns with the organization's risk appetite.

Placing KRIs in a logical framework will more clearly communicate status and highlight any area operating outside of the risk appetite and therefore requiring additional management focus. For example, if we're trying to determine whether we're responding well to incidents, our KRIs could include average response time, average containment time, and average remediation time, perhaps with trending of each. If the organization's risk appetite is "low," then each of these KRIs needs thresholds for "low" as well as for "medium" and "high." Performance should be in the "low" range, if that's your organization's stated appetite. Being temporarily in "medium" might be within risk tolerance but would require actions to address processes and controls to get back to "low" in the near term.

With KRIs in the categories of prevention, detection, and response, we have the main elements to understand if we're operating within risk appetite. To ensure that our current security posture is sustainable, we also need KRIs around whether we are keeping pace with the changing environment—skill sets, threat landscape, regulatory requirements, and so on.

A summary-level security dashboard aggregated from more detailed information offers a succinct way to communicate these KRIs and their status, color-coded with familiar red, yellow, and green (think traffic lights).

By presenting KRIs around detecting, preventing, responding, and awareness in this fashion and adding an executive summary with a few bullet points, you highlight key items of interest to leadership and bring focus to areas that need immediate attention.

The whole point of a dashboard that tells a complete and compelling story at a glance is to ensure that investments are being made in the right places and that capabilities and processes are implemented to protect the organization and its customers. An intuitive dashboard is a powerful tool in garnering sufficient attention and funding to ensure preparedness. Of course, that preparedness must be complemented by having the resources needed to rapidly respond to and remediate any incidents.

Once you have the answer to whether performance is within risk appetite—and the remediation plans to bring it back within the desired threshold, if not—then what? Where and how is this information used?

How to Engage in Governance and Oversight of Cyber Risk

The CISO of any organization where cyber is a critical risk should be actively engaged in the governance structure of the company. This structure may include subcommittees of an internal enterprise risk management committee that reports to the board of directors or to a subcommittee of the board. The overall structure might look something like Figure 6-1.

In order for the CISO to be engaged in the right places, he or she should consider in which corporate-level or enterprise committee(s) it would be appropriate to participate. If there is an overall enterprise risk management committee, it's vital that the CISO be a voting member. This level of participation gives CISOs visibility into and influence over the management of related and integrated risks such as business continuity and resiliency, third-party risk, reputation risk, and so on.

Though its name may vary, the enterprise risk management committee usually approves the organization's overall risk appetite statement, along

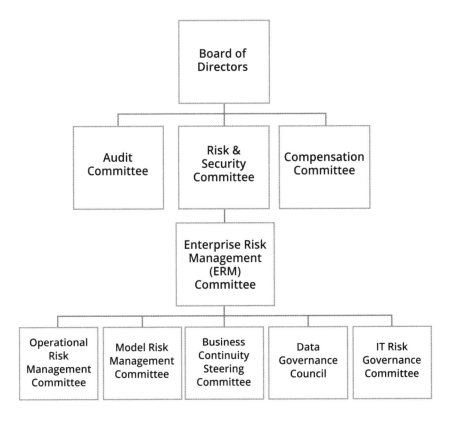

Figure 6-1. An organization chart for risk management

with any revisions to it. This committee is also tasked with understanding performance against the various risk appetite thresholds.

If cyber risk performance is outside of the risk appetite or, worse, outside of risk tolerance, the Enterprise Risk Management Committee, or its equivalent, would be the place the CISO would look for corporate direction and support. In addition to the ERM Committee, the CISO should also be a voting member of those few appropriate sub-committees, if they exist, focused on the other most critical risk areas, such as the Business Continuity Steering Committee and the IT Risk Governance Committee. The CISO should participate here to guide these critical programs, which are interwoven with and support the company's security posture, in order to ensure decisions and actions undertaken strengthen cyber risk management for the organization.

One area to call out specifically: if the organization has a Privacy Committee or a Privacy Office, it would be highly beneficial for the CISO to participate or have a close working relationship with this group. With a plethora of recent privacy regulations, combined with technology changes and the advances fraudsters have made, items to be considered relative to incident response and data and voice protection have expanded:

- It's now more likely that a security incident could also be a privacy incident with legal privacy requirements to satisfy.

- If there is a suspicion of an incident, consider engaging the Privacy and Legal departments immediately and discussing the appropriateness of working and communicating under attorney/client privilege. Also ensure that all work done will be supportive of satisfying legislative privacy requirements.

- There may be constraints against sharing with law enforcement as we have in the past, whether that's the data shared, when it's shared, or how and for what purpose it's shared.

How these incidents are handled has a great impact on a company's reputation so, here again, if the CISO has been engaged in the Business Continuity Steering Committee and has a comprehensive understanding of the entity's Crisis Management Plan and its structure, he or she will know how to engage this process and leverage it for the greatest success in handling events.

Other benefits of the CISO's active participation in governance committees include enabling the CISO to:

- Speak the language of integrated risk to the company's customers, regulators, and other key stakeholders

- Guide the company's view of cyber risk as a top risk for the organization

- Understand emerging risks in other areas that might have an impact on the cyber risk posture

- Demonstrate to external stakeholders effective oversight of the information security program and cyber risk

- Be an advocate for the business

Digital transformation, embedding of electronic interfaces in all products, virtualization, and other trends are going to continue to pick up speed and become even more pervasive. As a result, the CISO's strong and active engagement in their company's strategy development, governance structure, risk appetite statements, and integrated risk posture will become even more important. With an understanding of how the various risks are interwoven to impact a company's cyber risk posture, the CISO can be well positioned to vigorously support the achievement of corporate objectives.

With the understanding of where the CISO should plug in and how the overall cyber risk program should be measured, overseen, and governed, the question is now "Have the right cyber risks been brought forward to inform the governance and oversight process?" Leveraging the risk management life cycle to identify, assess, manage, remediate, and report risk will enable a full understanding of your cybersecurity posture.

Thinking Strategically About Potential Risks

As the CISO works with his or her team to understand which risks should be managed and reported on, it's important to use a wide lens and think strategically.

Historically, identified risks have included items very specific to the information security program such as vulnerabilities, cyberattacks, and insider threats. These types of risks still need to be measured and monitored.

But, as previously mentioned, the role of the CISO has become much broader and so areas of potential contribution to the organization by the CISO broaden commensurately.

As a result, risks to the organization from the cyber perspective should also include strategic considerations like:

- The risk of maintaining a fully staffed security program when security professionals are in enormously short supply

- The risk that security staff skill sets are not updated in alignment with the organization's changing technology and priorities

- The risk of insufficient agility for operating in a totally new environment, such as with the rapid and massive transition to work from home due to COVID-19, or the movement into wholly new business areas

- The risk that the organization's information security program won't keep up and remain effective in the face of rapidly evolving threats

In order to ensure consistently strong and comprehensive risk management in information security, the CISO should consider establishing a risk management group within his or her organization to assist with systematically managing risks such as these. An effective risk management program would encompass:

- Skilled risk managers
- Appropriate tools and processes for identifying, assessing, mitigating, and reporting risks
- A specific emerging/strategic risk component
- Strong governance that includes appropriate policies and procedures and an oversight structure to ensure not only compliance but satisfaction of all risk and business requirements

As risks are identified and evaluated, both the likelihood and the potential impact of the risk materializing in your organization need to be determined so that you can develop a remediation plan. The higher the likelihood and potential impact, the higher that risk needs to be on your list of priorities.

As you consider various risks, don't lose sight of the fact that to be strategic, you must also be agile. Not all risks are going to be known at any given time, which is why your risk management program should include an emerging/strategic component. As members of the US Marines are fond of saying, "Adapt and overcome." Cyber is ever evolving, and in order to survive the "fog of war," you will need to build flexible risk mitigation strategies that support your business needs.

As an example, considering the worldwide shortage of trained cybersecurity personnel, most organizations will determine the likelihood of remaining fully staffed is low and the impact of not doing so is high. This is clearly a risk that should be addressed.

In creating a remediation plan to share with the Enterprise Risk Management Committee and other stakeholders, consider a multi-pronged approach to solving the problem. This should include "growing your own" through external partnerships with local schools and colleges, including STEM programs and internships.

Of course, it also includes building on internal resources. These internal resources could include employees in IT and other risk organizations where personnel have transferable skills and might have an interest in moving over to information security. Another option to consider may be embedding security skills into the various work streams instead of consolidating the team under a single cyber risk division.

There is no single approach that is the perfect fit for every organization. To be most effective, it's important to select an approach that meets the needs of your individual organization.

For example, many public-sector organizations struggle with obtaining appropriate funding for highly skilled individuals. Those that operate in areas of close proximity to tech hubs are generally on the losing end of any employment sourcing opportunities. If you are in environments similar to this where employment is a struggle, think less about creating a cyber "kingdom" and more about load balancing cyber throughout the various IT operations. For more details on this topic, see Chapter 5, "Addressing the Skills and Diversity Gap."

Reducing Risk by Sharing Information

Information sharing is arguably one of the most important aspects of reducing risk. To best guard against today's world of evolving risks and threats, we must share quickly and openly with those in similar business sectors as well as with other industries. The US Department of Homeland Security has classified sixteen industries as "critical infrastructure" sectors.[1]

Most sectors have Information Sharing and Analysis Centers (ISACs) or Information Sharing and Analysis Organizations (ISAOs). These groups exist solely for mutual support of like organizations by expeditious sharing of cyber threats and incidents as well as best practices. If your organization is not a member, strongly consider joining one of these valuable groups.

In addition, it is highly recommended that you look to partner with other entities within your area. All state governments and some local governments participate in private-public sharing.[2] Becoming a member of a sharing organization provides a different view into the current threat landscape and best practices across multiple sectors. Additionally, some federal agencies share information, like the FBI which hosts InfraGard,[3] another method for cross-sector collaboration.

Another point to take into consideration is how to share data. Many organizations today are hesitant to share data related to cyber incidents out of fear that if released, it may impact their reputation. This is an understandable and valid concern. The information-sharing framework must allow for anonymization of the submitter (if requested). In addition, only pertinent data such as indicators of compromise (IOCs) should be shared.

Building a collaborative relationship with local government or other external entities can sometimes be challenging. Generally in order to establish and maintain a relationship, there must first be trust. Unfortunately trust often takes time, and in today's world, time is not always available. In cases where there is resistance to building trust, there are two main options: to force change through legislation or mandate or to enable change using a combination of a "carrot method" and other offers of assistance. These options should be considered on a case-by-case basis. It is not always advisable to use mandates and legislation to get a desired effect. Attempting to legislate change may lead to a counterintuitive situation where granular and often pertinent information is not shared.

What has been successful in some cases when working with external entities is establishing partnerships and offering solutions that will reduce their cyber risks. This may be done through offering support in the form of SME consultations and/or physical support to aid a cyber-impacted organization. Other times, it may be appropriate to formalize the actions with a mandate or through legislation, but it is advisable to work on building the relationship first before taking this route.

Many states are actively implementing ways to reduce risk through the adoption of a "whole-of-state" approach to information sharing. Whole-of-state means looking past authoritative boundaries established by laws and adopting a more cohesive strategy based on partnerships across private, public, and academic channels.

In North Carolina, for example, the state has established programs to support local government and schools in their response to cyber incidents. This is only one of a myriad of support mechanisms in place. The "big picture" for the state is the overall protection of a resident's data. This data is not only stored in state agency systems, but is also housed within local counties, municipalities, and schools. In addition, much of the critical infrastructure supporting the state resides at the local government level. These are systems that provide critical services such as 911, water, power, and others, often supported with limited resources and funding. By establishing a whole-of-state approach, North Carolina is able to adopt a team approach and build relationships and partnerships of trust and mutual support.

How can you apply this concept in your organization? The first step is to understand the situation and resources at your disposal. The North Carolina Department of IT accomplished this by first conducting a strength, weakness, opportunity, and threat (SWOT) analysis. They identified key stakeholders such as local government information technology and cyber professionals who can be assembled to support any impacted parties within the state's government structure. Over time, a solid foundation of trust is built, which further enables information sharing. IOCs, best practices, and other pertinent information can be quickly disseminated statewide to ensure all potential targets are protected. Anyone can leverage this same approach by networking and building relationships to call on in times of need, strengthening the entire ecosystem.

Information sharing is an important strategy for mitigating today's threats; see Chapter 4 for more information on this topic.

Reducing Risk Through Cyber Insurance

Does cyber insurance make sense as a risk reduction strategy? It might not make much sense to buy cyber insurance if resources are still lacking for purchasing and implementing solutions to support needed security controls. But cyber insurance does have a role to play.

As the rest of this chapter makes clear, we do not recommend that you rely solely on cyber insurance. Doing so is reckless and a poor approach to risk management. In fact, having cyber insurance does not shift any of the ownership and accountability for risk, which remains fully with the organization that purchases the insurance. Instead, cyber insurance should be looked at as another tool within an organization's risk toolbox. Cyber insurance offers both the customer and the company a means to reduce cost implications from a cyber breach by paying first-party costs associated with a breach, such as forensics, victim notification, and credit card monitoring.

Another potential rationale for purchasing cyber insurance is to gain external confirmation that an organization has leveraged a standard approach to implementing a security program. Many reputable sellers of cyber insurance require that their customers meet, at a minimum, cyber best practices prior to being sold a policy. These best practices are aligned to industry frameworks such as the NIST Cybersecurity Framework.[4]

If you have a small business, cyber insurance may well be worth the cost. Statistically, over 60% of small businesses impacted by cyber incidents fail to recover.[5] Given the fact that cyber breaches and incidents continue to grow in size and sophistication, this option should be considered a part of the cost of doing business.

In Closing

The CISO role today requires a strong strategic thinker who can be not only a collaborative partner for the business but also a strategic partner to other risk organizations. Having strong relationships across the organization and with key external consortia enables a stronger risk posture for the entire enterprise. Being embedded in the risk oversight and governance processes, armed with an informative set of KRIs plus understanding of the full universe of potentially impactful risks from a broad viewpoint, allows the CISO to be a leader in ensuring the success of the organization's objectives.

Notes

1. https://www.cisa.gov/critical-infrastructure-sectors
2. https://us-cert.cisa.gov/resources/sltt
3. https://www.infragard.org/
4. https://www.nist.gov/cyberframework
5. https://www.vox.com/sponsored/11196054/why-every-small-business-should-care-about-cyber-attacks-in-5-charts

SUZANNE HARTIN

Suzanne Hartin is Chief Risk Officer for Early Warning. In this role, she leads the company's risk functions including information security, privacy, enterprise and operational risk management, business continuity and crisis management, third-party risk management, compliance, and physical security.

Suzanne has more than twenty years of risk management experience developed at a variety of the nation's largest financial institutions. Prior to joining Early Warning, she was Vice President of Operational Risk Management at Capital One where she managed the Enterprise Business Continuity and Crisis Management teams as well as the Corporate Third Party Risk Management and Corporate Insurance Risk Management programs. She has also held a number of executive risk, compliance, and information security positions at American Express and Bank of America.

Suzanne graduated from Davidson College with a degree in economics. She is a Certified Information Security Manager (CISM) and is certified in Risk and Information Systems Control (CRISC). Suzanne serves on the Board of Directors for Sytek Electric, the world leader in design and manufacture of high-powered sub-sea motors used on ROVs (remotely operated vehicles) and other sub-sea applications and is a member of ISACA and the Executive Women's Forum (EWF).

MARIA S. THOMPSON

Maria S. Thompson joined the North Carolina Department of Information Technology in January 2015 as the state's first chief risk officer, reporting to the state chief information officer. This position was established as part of the state's efforts to bring information risk management capabilities in line with industry standards.

In her role, Thompson is responsible for developing an integrated statewide framework to manage information risk, including operations, security, and data protection.

She comes to NCDIT with decades of IT security experience. She began her career with twenty years of service in the US Marine Corps and retired as the cybersecurity chief for the Marine Corps. Her previous roles include serving as the Iraq Theater of Operations Certification Authority. She also served as a senior security engineer for SecureInfo and senior security architect and program manager for Imperatis Corp. in Virginia.

Thompson holds an MS in information technology from University of Maryland University College (UMUC).

7
Blending NOC and SOC

MEL T. MIGRIÑO

W HEN YOUR SECURITY TEAM FACES A DISRUPTIVE incident, time is of the essence. Any delay in identifying, responding to, and mitigating the problem increases risks and leads to still more disruption. These costly delays are more likely in entities where the Network Operations Center (NOC) and Security Operations Center (SOC) are completely separate with limited visibility into the other's world. When teams remain siloed, inefficiencies and errors slow effective incident response and hamper overall network and security operations.

As cyber threats continue to increase in number and severity, siloed NOC and SOC teams are a luxury your organization cannot afford. But as we'll see, the solution is not necessarily a quick, complete blending or merger of the two teams. Failing to consider all the details of blending or rushing to complete the process can create additional problems without necessarily solving the issues at hand. A more nuanced answer is required.

The Vision

Just as firefighters and emergency medical technicians together respond to fires and work in tandem to both put out fires and treat victims, integrated SOC and NOC response teams can work together to troubleshoot incidents and keep the network both secure and reliable. Key benefits of blending NOC and SOC include:

- Faster resolution of incidents. Instead of working independently after an incident occurs and sometimes reaching conflicting conclusions as to the root cause, blended teams can quickly identify a problem, track the causes, and thoroughly mitigate and solve the issue.

- Reduced system downtime. With teams working effectively and rapidly in tandem, security incidents are less likely to develop into prolonged network disruptions.

- Reduced incident impact. By addressing incidents holistically and collaboratively using a playbook defined and practiced in advance, a blended NOC and SOC shuts down incidents faster and thereby reduces their damaging effects.

- Improved processes. Co-locating or blending teams makes it easier to launch an integrated incident investigation.

- Increased information sharing. Team members who know each other are more likely to share information both formally and informally. This information sharing can lead to thinking outside the box and result in insight that leads to improvements.

- Knowledge across areas. Co-located teams understand how the other team members work, how they approach problems, and why certain requirements are in place. This increased understanding improves incident response, daily operations, and long-term business success.

- Better coordination with other relevant teams. A blended team, especially if there is a single point person, can more easily coordinate with additional groups as needed.

- More effective use of emerging technology, automation, and tools. With more alignment, more work can be automated. Automation is most helpful for teams that are aligned. If the NOC and SOC are siloed, it is hard to automate best practices or use AI to identify threats. Tools can be jointly tuned so that they produce optimal results, such as accurate alerts versus false positives or under alerting. As more work is automated, overworked analysts can focus on higher-value tasks.

- Fewer dashboards. The resulting dashboards include indicators relevant to both teams.

- More frequent and cohesive training and tabletop exercises. These exercises build response expertise and team integration.

The Danger of Blending Superficially or Too Quickly

The benefits of blending NOC and SOC are clear. But the devil is in the details. A 50-50 merger is hard to guarantee. In a merger, one culture often prevails over the other. If the NOC perspective wins, your organization ends up with a highly available, insecure network. If the SOC mindset prevails, your network is highly secure, but access is more restricted.

If the transition is rushed, it is not well executed, and/or either team assumes the responsibilities of the other team without proper planning, the following issues will likely occur:

- Incorrect analysis of security incidents by NOC and incidents are not fully resolved.

- Prolonged and incomplete analysis of debug logs by SOC and native network-related incidents are not assessed properly and resolved.

- Varying execution of change management process and approvals with resulting confusion.

- Security and/or network activities executed without knowledge and familiarity, resulting in delayed support to end users.

NOC and SOC Focus on Different Issues

To understand how to avoid mistakes and successfully knit NOC and SOC capabilities together, we must understand the differences between the mindset of each team.

In ongoing operations and during disruptive incidents, NOC and SOC, by necessity, focus on different issues. When a problem occurs, each side deploys its own response team—often using duplicative tools and looking through two different lenses at the same set of data. Not surprisingly, the network team approaches incidents from a network availability standpoint while the security team approaches the same issues from the perspective of malicious intent or security vulnerabilities. What appears to be a network problem actually may be an attack or another cyber issue; and what looks like a cyber incident or threat may in reality be a network issue. Some issues fall into both categories.

NOC and SOC meet at the firewall, which is important to both teams. Each team, however, has different skills, different concerns, and even different reasons for caring about the firewall.

NOC is focused on availability, reliability, and management of network devices including switches, routers, wired and wireless lines, laptops, tablets, load balancers, and firewalls. A major focus is defining firewall policies. The NOC side of the house also monitors all network traffic, the availability of devices on the network, and capacity thresholds. In the event of a problem, the NOC team looks closely at the debug logs and focuses on network device troubleshooting. Team members study debug logs to determine what specifically is wrong with a switch, a firewall, or something else on the network.

Meantime, the SOC team focuses more narrowly overall on monitoring suspicious or malicious activities and IP addresses. Instead of all the debug logs, the SOC team wants normalized logs that correspond to specific IPs, dates, and timestamps. Instead of firewall policies, the SOC team wants to know how its next-gen (NG) firewall responded in real time to a potential attack: Did an alert go out, or was the threat trapped in the NG firewall? A SOC incident investigation starts with root-cause analysis and proceeds to digital forensics focusing on threat behavior analysis/malware analysis. The SOC investigating team also covers end-to-end damage recovery and remediation.

As for the bigger picture, the SOC team is empowered to review general network policies, formulate security policies governing network connections and integrations, and approve specific connections to the network. Any changes in the network architecture and deviation from network security policies must pass through a SOC risk assessment that recommends alternate controls to manage the risks.

After a disruptive event, the two teams may reach divergent conclusions and send conflicting recommendations to management. The result: the triggering issue takes too long to solve, teams are frustrated, and leadership (the source of your budget!) is also frustrated. Multiply that frustration by hundreds of security incidents and the result is an overarching disconnect between the two teams, more opportunities for threat actors, and less support from an organization's leadership. Working to improve cooperation and collaboration between the two teams while keeping their differing perspectives in mind is the key to success.

Approaches to Blending NOC and SOC

In companies where the NOC and SOC are siloed, the people and change management issues surrounding this merger must be addressed. Each group has its favorite tools and processes; meshing them will not happen overnight, if ever. Each center also has its own budget, its own set of leaders, and its own organizational structure. Ideally, a blended NOC and SOC results in improved operations of both the network and security.

Organizations take different approaches to achieve increased collaboration and blending.

Some organizations create a single entity such as a Cyber Fusion Center or Integrated Operations Center. Combined centers often include the cloud operations team. Depending on the threat landscape and risk appetite of the organization, a complete blending of NOC and SOC, with both under the CISO, may be a favorable approach.

Organizations that are highly risk conscious would prefer to settle for separate teams under the CISO organization for a unified process on change management and approvals and alignment of policies and standards while instilling security and availability. However, if the full transition of the NOC to the CISO organization is not properly structured to ensure segregation of duties, the mandate of the SOC, which is to monitor and block suspicious or malicious traffic, may not prevail because the (mostly desired) emerging culture of trust between NOC and SOC could lead to problems. For example, NOC would have the capability to adjust the network bandwidth to achieve network goals, and SOC may skip policing any suspicious traffic because of the developing camaraderie between the teams.

An easy-to-manage approach is for teams to remain under different leadership organizations of the CIO and CISO but to work in proximity to achieve cohesive collaboration and faster time to respond.

Other organizations may keep traditional organizational operations but co-locate teams not necessarily in the same room but in the same facility; call it managed proximity.

Breaking Down Silos to Build Teams

Breaking down different mentalities and approaches to problems can be difficult. Collaboration is not the first instinct for many people with technical skills. When they see a problem, their first instinct is to try to solve it and to solve it alone. Encouraging a collaboration-first mentality is a challenge.

But once in place, collaboration reduces finger pointing between teams. Instead of worrying about whose problem it is and seeking to lay the task on the other team, the blended or collaborating team now works together to solve the issue at hand. This puts the emphasis where it belongs: on rapidly resolving the incident and reducing its impact.

The culture you establish is also important (a topic covered in more detail in Chapter 3). Systems over-alert, but people rarely do. Often tier 1 analysts may not want to raise a particular issue for fear of bothering leadership. Encourage staff to raise issues early so that you can assess them rather than waiting to confirm issues themselves before reporting.

Especially if the teams remain somewhat separate, create clear, formal communication channels between your NOC and SOC teams. But also create environments that enable casual sharing of information and insight between the two teams. Perhaps a shared kitchen or water cooler.

Working with Executive Leadership

General counsel, the chief risk officer, CEOs, and CIOs are very concerned about risk; improper incident handling can result in court cases. The legal and risk teams offer guidance for handling incidents so that the organization can stay out of court if possible or be properly prepared if an incident results in legal proceedings.

Proactively, CISOs should consult these groups to ensure that policies and procedures stay within legal frameworks. See Chapter 2 for more information on communicating with the board.

Processes for Integrating the NOC and SOC

Change management is a big piece of blending the NOC and SOC, but, as with any initiative, the metrics you choose matter. Instead of volume-based security metrics, mature organizations concentrate on impact-based metrics and trends linked to certain types of attacks, security gaps, and misconfigured controls.

Developing best practices will help you blend the NOC and SOC to create a better security defense. In addition to best practices, create clear and detailed playbooks so teams know what plan of action to follow during a threat event. Make sure you have playbooks tailored to each type of incident, as steps vary depending on the type of incident you are dealing with.

Then, supplement your playbooks with one-pagers or cheat sheets that your team members can quickly reference. These cheat sheets should include information such as which alerts matter, how to respond initially, and when and to whom to escalate an issue.

Assigning responsibilities is another key process. For example, NOC can lead Level 1 monitoring, but the skills and responsibility for investigating incidents are best assumed by the SOC team. Meanwhile, network monitoring is something SOC team members can learn, but NOC should lead network troubleshooting because that is their domain of expertise.

Keep in mind, however, that there is no holy grail structure for stronger collaboration and cooperation between NOC and SOC. The emerging structure is going to be different in every organization.

Tabletop Exercises

Organizations can better respond to attacks and other cyber incidents when they have prepared and rehearsed beforehand. Tabletop exercises are a key way to train analysts, rehearse responses to threat events, and promote cohesion among NOC and SOC team members.

Such events should include a variety of stakeholders; you may need people from legal, human resources, and corporate communications as well as business owners to provide system or scenario context. Look to hold a major daylong tabletop exercise once or twice a year and shorter, focused events quarterly if possible.

Incident Review

Playbooks, cheat sheets, tabletop exercises, and ongoing training are all important, but nothing replaces an after-the-fact incident review. In this review, teams seek to answer questions such as: Did this threat create an alert? If not, why not? If so, why didn't we respond?

Organizations can use this information in their incident response plans to better train analysts so they can understand why an incident happened. A threat event should not be the first time team members see the response protocols. Based on the findings, materials and systems can be updated to alert analysts earlier in the threat cycle.

Sharing Threat Information with Peers

The only way to prepare for incidents is to anticipate them. This requires staying abreast of the latest threats. Just as attackers share malware and exploits among themselves, CISOs also need to be engaged and share threat information with counterparts in their industries.

Stay informed about current threats by asking questions like:

- What are the current threat trends?
- Is ransomware on the rise in your sector?
- If so, what kinds of ransomware?
- Does the ransomware exhibit certain behaviors you can track?

This sharing among your peers at other organizations will help you understand what types of attacks are hitting your sector and who the actors are. You can make sure you have the right controls to address their tactics, techniques, and procedures. By becoming part of a community of interest or other information-sharing channel, you can get ahead of activity that could trend and become a nightmare for your organization.

Highlighting Critical Issues

Existing security tools generate too many alerts and voluminous logs. Some solutions offer a way to correlate alerts across systems and reduce the number of alerts. If we think of the NOC and SOC as frontline workers like firefighters and EMTs, alerts should indicate real emergencies or at least the equivalent of a beeping smoke detector.

Right now, at many organizations, a preponderance of false positives makes it hard to find real issues. Even when systems alert only on genuine issues, the task for analysts is working to find the issues with the most impact. It is not even like finding a needle in a haystack; it's like trying to find a dirty needle in a stack of needles. Especially with so-called low and slow attacks becoming more prevalent and attacker dwell times rising, significant long-term breaches may fail to alert anyone or may appear as minor and easily dismissed alerts.

Technology for Improved Incident Response

Organizations are awash in data and alerts, partly because of the sheer number of security tools in use. Too often, each tool is designed to act independently, producing its own logs and alerts and making it difficult to correlate information across tools.

Tier 1 analysts do not have years of experience and may not know which playbook or even cheat sheet to reach for. And in trying to prove themselves, they may not ask for help. (See most disaster movies for missteps like these.)

When custom tooling is needed to bridge these gaps, security analysts should be consulted throughout the development cycle. Too often, security analysts provide requirements for an application they want from engineering, and then engineering teams make a judgment call and ignore some of the requirements. The resulting product is ineffective and, instead of being deployed, ends up in the land of broken toys, which is a waste of everyone's time.

Emerging commercial solutions help with some urgent needs for the NOC and SOC.

One recent category of tools that is important for the NOC and SOC is called *secure orchestration automation and response (SOAR)*. A SOAR takes alerts, prioritizes them, and contextualizes them with relevant elements of your playbooks so that information on critical next steps is provided along with alerts.

SOARs, like many modern security tools, use AI and machine learning to sift through voluminous data, identify patterns that are anomalous, and pull in contextual information. SOAR systems use this to present analysts with concrete and relevant information in a timely manner so that the analysts can effectively respond to incidents.

This is one of many examples of letting machines do what they do best (sorting through large volumes of data) and letting people do what they do best (investigating and acting on information). Experienced personnel help tune such systems so that they improve and yield better results for analysts running the integrated NOC and SOC.

A Smooth but Slow Transition

NOC and SOC can work well together if leadership and teams exercise appropriate delineation of responsibilities, adopt good technology, and establish sound policies. But remember: Rushing leads to risks and regrets. Regardless of the transition model, adequate time for knowledge transfer and training must be allowed. Usually six to twelve months will be enough. This can be extended depending on the results.

Normally after the training, NOC can assume SOC Level 1 support and monitoring. However, forensics, which is a specialized skill, remains a SOC domain. In the same way, the SOC team can assume the network monitoring and initial triage, but in-depth analysis of the debug logs may really take time. Plan for a one-year transition.

Some type of blending, or at the very least, collaboration, is the direction the industry is heading. But the best approach is like driving on a curvy, mountainous road: proceed with extreme caution. Collaborate, cooperate, and blend slowly. Test the road and keep looking ahead before moving too quickly. It's better to live with a little bit of tension than with a failed merger.

If you keep the potential dangers, details, and differences in mind, you can slowly but successfully blend the two teams or establish a new normal of increased collaboration and cooperation.

MEL T. MIGRIÑO

Mel T. Migriño is the Chairperson and President of the Women in Security Alliance Philippines (WiSAP), an organization that focuses on empowering and inspiring women in security. Mel is listed among Women to Watch on RiskyWomen.org and was recognized as a top 20 IFSEC Global Influencer in the Security Executives category. She is a regular contributor to Women in Security Magazine.

Mel has more than fifteen years of combined experience in information security management, cybersecurity governance, assurance and operations, application and infrastructure security, operational technology (OT) security, cloud security, business continuity, IT disaster recovery, enterprise risk management, privacy, IT audit, and project management across multiple industries. Currently, Mel is the Vice President and Group CISO of a power distribution conglomerate in the Philippines. Formerly, she served as the cybersecurity leader of a Big Four auditing firm and the largest fintech firm in the Philippines.

8

Security by Design
Strategies for a Shift-Left Culture

ANNE MARIE ZETTLEMOYER

H ACKER SUMMER CAMP IS AN ANNUAL WEEKLONG TREK into the blistering heat of Las Vegas in August where more than 10,000 security pros and fans gather to rub elbows, share ideas, and reconnect over a series of security conferences, mainly BsidesLV, DEF CON, and Black Hat. It's a family reunion of sorts, where memories are made (and forgotten) and ideas are formed, argued, developed, and matured.

It was at this event a few years ago where I had conversation after conversation around security by design—DevSecOps to some (security should be in the definition!), definitely not DevSecOps for others (DevOps must be held pure!), and to all the endeavor to "shift left" and bring security to the beginning of the development process versus bolting it on at the end. It's the noble effort to include "secure" in the definition of quality and "safe" in the definition of ready and to do so efficiently and effectively throughout the product life cycle. Whether you're a DevOps purist or a DevSecOps advocate, despite the many debates on labels, we can all agree that the things we create should be safe and stay safe for as long as they are in use.

Obviously...right?

If you've ventured into the space of application security or security by design, you'll have seen that the notion of securing something up front is many times met with a lot of head nodding (oh yes, that's a great idea!), only to result in even more head shaking when speed of development overtakes the priority of compliance or security (oh wait, you meant now?).

You may have heard a series of relatable and somewhat understandable lamentations like:

- "All these rules slow us down."
- "We just want to iterate to an MVP to prove the value."
- "But we passed the audit already. We'll deal with that later."
- "You security folks are just spreading FUD. It's fine!"

and my favorite:

- "It just has to work!"

By this point, I see security pros experience a plethora of reactions—including disbelief, frustration, throwing hands up, and maybe even some weeping or full-on carb bingeing. Why? Because it's frustrating to have good intentions fall through, but I can tell you this: those developers are diving into their feelings on the other side too.

The result? We spin our wheels, relying on expensive near-production or post-production assessments or alerts like pen-tests, bug bounties, and the dreaded "incident" to reveal problem areas. As a result, the business ends up spending ten or eleven times more on fixing security flaws found "at the end" than it would have had we worked together more effectively up front. That doesn't include the costs of a compromise or breach.

So, what can we do differently?

In this chapter, I'll share my experiences across industries and dive into methods and ideas on how to establish a secure development culture and build the partnerships in order to create securely *by design*.

What Is Secure Development? What Does It Encompass?

Before diving into strategies, let's define our terms.

Secure application development includes both secure coding and secure practices. As mentioned earlier, "secure" must be part of the definition of quality and functional acceptance. It's not enough to focus on writing secure code; writing the code is just one part of the development life cycle.

We have to put equal emphasis on maintaining the safety and security standard for quality by investing in people (both skill and capacity) as well as achieving and maintaining proper hygiene of the product along with the infrastructure it sits on and interacts with. We need to make space for tech refresh, remediation of vulnerabilities, and required upgrades as systems, products, and infrastructure age. Like most things, it's a combination of people, process, and technology that makes the magic work ... in that order.

Skipping Ahead to Process and Technology—Wait, What?

It's true that everything starts with people, and we'll spend the most time exploring strategies on how to hack that part of the people-process-technology triad. However, since we're still talking about definitions, let's get a few things out of the way.

Fit for Purpose and Scale

I'll start out by saying that not all of this is going to apply to everything your company develops. How you harden your products and approach security by design must be appropriate for your product's threat landscape and your business's risk appetite. The strategies in this chapter are meant to provide ideas on how to approach some of the tougher problems in implementing a secure-by-design culture, but there is not a one-size-fits-all methodology. Not every product needs the same frequency or level of scrutiny, and deciding what "fit for purpose and scale" means will change for products as well as the business over time.

That said, there are some key components of testing and tools that make security by design easier and more successful for many. Let's talk about a few of those components.

Findings by People

While many types of testing can be automated, a few require humans to take the lead.

Design Review and Threat Modeling

Usually done by a security engineer (hopefully embedded in the product or development team), this component helps the team think through how things can go wrong. What are the possible misuses of the technology? What weak points are introduced into the business's ecosystem through its development or connectivity? When done regularly and across business units, this process also helps inform the security organization's strategy on what capabilities and functions are needed to keep up with business needs.

Threat modeling is time-intensive. If resources are scarce, it should be prioritized for the highest risk or most valuable assets and programs at a frequency that makes sense for decision-making. Regular security engineering reviews should be slated throughout the development process and may include activities like reviewing technical architecture documents, interpreting security findings, and approving remediation plans.

Penetration Tests and Bug Bounty Programs

These tests find vulnerabilities by emulating how an attacker might interact with and compromise an application, infrastructure, or system. Penetration tests should be done pre-production and are often required by various compliance standards and regulations. Bug bounty programs are structured agreements on how to handle and reward responsible vulnerability disclosure for researchers who test products postproduction.

Findings by Tools

Scanners embedded in the integrated development environment (IDE) can be useful in catching errors early on in the process and ideally provide timely feedback to the developer on weak coding practices. Static application security testing (SAST) tools focus on the lines of code and can help validate source code and third-party libraries as well as regularly scan both for insecure practices and known vulnerabilities. Dynamic application security testing (DAST) tools look for weaknesses while the app is running (usually web apps and services), and integrated application security testing (IAST) is meant to combine the goals of both but in more modern infrastructures. All of these tools require a level of hygiene in the application and the tool itself to be effective.

Process Is Very Important

Successful implementation not only incorporates timely feedback for the developer, but it also heavily relies on regular tuning and quality checks on the tool itself to guard against a flood of false positives and the apathy that creates. Failing to invest in validating the quality of these scans can end up in wasted investment and more "noise" that goes unactioned, leaving potentially serious issues to go unnoticed and allowing risk to accumulate.

Define Value Up Front

It's also helpful to define the goals for using these tools. Each tool has limitations and should not be used as a "point and scan" solution alone. Many companies find it hard to get value from these tools because they fail to invest time in defining the goals for each tool and configuring the tools to meet those goals. SAST tools are notorious for too many findings (false positives); DAST tools can have coverage problems or fail to manage the complexity of an app and "not find enough." It should not be expected that any one technology will find everything that is important and nothing that isn't.

If the goal is help uncover some problem areas at a faster pace and wider scale than a human can, or to help shift some of the testing capabilities to trained and supported engineering teams, these tools can be very useful by enabling scale and speed of testing. For organizations with very limited resources, tools can provide coverage where there might not be any otherwise.

Many bug bounty reports find common weaknesses that could have been found by more automated processes. There's a reason why cross-site scripting and injection vulnerabilities remain on the OWASP Top 10[1] every year—but it's a not a good one. We keep making the same mistakes in the development process over and over again.

Using tools earlier in the product life cycle can uncover known vulnerabilities like these and provide feedback to the developers to help decrease repeat errors over time. These patterns should be monitored and measured and part of the feedback loop to communicate efficacy of the programs and tools—but more on that later.

The Bottom Line

Tools have an essential place in the security-by-design journey when met with robust processes and skilled teams. You still need knowledgeable humans to tune the tools, interpret the findings, and, of course, fix them.

People

Speaking of knowledgeable humans, it all starts with people. With one exception...

It's Not All About You

It's actually not even *mostly* about you. It's about the business and what they are trying to achieve, and it's about the customers and the safety they expect and deserve. As security pros, we are here to enable the business to achieve their goals safely. If the business is a race car, we are the brake; we are the pit crew when needed—there to fix, diagnose problems, and radio the driver so they know when it's safe to hit the gas as well as inform them of potential threats and risks. We are the emergency response team when something really goes wrong.

Now before you cringe at the brake analogy, consider this. A key enabler of a car's ability to go faster than a snail's pace is the presence and functionality of the brake. Without it, a car could not safely operate, and drivers would be stuck with a very slow and very frustrating user experience. The brake is what gives the car the flexibility to slow down when, where, and how it is needed to get the driver where they want to go. It allows for heavier materials and more robust builds and features. A brake by itself? A cool, albeit excessive, paperweight. But a brake as part of a multi-layered safety system? That's an enabler of the ultimate in driver experience and vehicle performance. We are here to enable the business.

Get to Know Who It *Is* About

Aside from really understanding the business you're protecting and the proposed product or service you're assessing (get cozy with the 10-K and the 8-K SEC forms[2] if you have them), spend some time understanding the role and day job of the developers and engineers who are building this stuff. Remember that designing solutions for the business also means designing for how the business operates, not just its goals.

How do the developers work? How are they incentivized? What are their views on security, and how does it affect them? If you've heard some of the quotes from the beginning of this chapter, you probably have a few guesses, but ask anyway. So much can be gained in both insight and cooperation by practicing empathy and genuinely seeking to understand the world development teams have to create in. Listen to their experiences and aim to craft solutions that create as little friction for the developer experience as possible; even better is to co-create the solution with them. The key to getting buy-in is making sure the other side feels heard, valued, and understood.

The goal is to embed security into the design, where not only are we working alongside the creation efforts, but we're also teaching and evangelizing the principles of security so that we get better at creating—safely, with fewer defects at each iteration.

Lead with Empathy

Get intentional and genuine in the discovery and partnership process.

It's not a secret that security can have a dreaded reputation. Years of "Thou shalts" and "Thou shall nots" are hurdles we have to acknowledge and overcome. One strategy for building bridges and investing in people and connections is to create opportunities for individuals and teams to come together in a casual and genuine way.

Sponsoring small activities that empower your team to engage with other teams is golden. Encourage them to treat partners to one-on-one coffees or small group lunches to help folks get to know each other as people and colleagues. These simple connections can pay large dividends in forming the partnerships needed to tackle the tough stuff down the road and not just with developers and engineering teams. It takes all kinds of disciplines and partnerships to make this work. That means including finance, product development, marketing, legal, HR, operations, technology, and so on. The key here is to provide space, resources, and the expectation to do these things. As a leader, you can empower your team by allocating thirty minutes every other week or month for relationship-building activities and pave the way for engagement by working with the leaders of other organizations to do the same.

Successful implementation relies on an opt-in method rather than forced participation. Opt-in results in more engaging connections and allows for flexibility for personal preference, schedules, and working styles. Your goal here is to create the opportunity to be intentional about forming relationships between teams, not forcing people to talk to each other.

Have geo-diverse teams? Casual virtual coffees or lunches can be very effective proxies for the serendipity enjoyed by on-site teams bumping into each other in the halls. Get creative and order a favorite coffee drink or an inexpensive lunch delivered to each participant and watch the ideas spark over lattes or a slice.

Skill Up for Scale

Teach 'em to fish. That's fish—not phish.

One of the bigger gripes I hear from engineering teams is that they aren't clear on what security expects of them. "Just tell me what to do," they say.

It seems simple, but security teams fail at this all the time. We overcomplicate and cite rules instead of teaching principles, measuring, and providing feedback on performance. We stop short of explaining the "why" and fail to contextualize findings or explain threat models in relatable terms. We deploy tools that produce too much data or too many false positives for anyone to understand or act on, resulting in alert fatigue and apathy. We talk in "what-ifs" to engineering teams who are used to working in binary terms—the code works or it doesn't; the light turns on or it doesn't. What-ifs are met with eye rolls. The reality is, both sides need to do something different to get different results.

We need to become really good teachers, storytellers, and coaches. The latest industry ratios are about 100:1 for developers to security engineers—and that's for companies that have invested in the process.

The bottom line: There will never be enough security engineers to go around. We can't possibly look at everything. We need to multiply our skill sets and mindsets across developer populations to scale security knowledge and efforts. This means realizing that most in-seat developers are not taught security principles or secure coding practices as a core part of the curriculum. It also means that many don't realize or have not been educated in "the art of the possible" when it comes to security concerns.

We often forget that while many of us live and breathe this stuff, most other folks do not. The impact of an incident is not usually top of mind until it happens, and the resulting interest will wane over time. This is starting to change as engineering curriculums evolve; however, chances are that the folks in the seats right now could use a hand figuring out what to do. And no, that does not mean relying on the annual thirty-minute security compliance training. We can all have an eye roll at that.

Secure Code Training—Up Front and Then Some

I've been in eight industries and worked with over twenty organizations either in-house or as a consultant. In all of those scenarios, what I remember most— even from experiences decades ago—is the orientation and onboarding process. It set the tone for the business, set the expectations of work, and fostered close relationships with folks who started on the same day as I did. Our shared experience of the first day, the "class of" if you will, helped build relationships that persist even now—years down the road.

In one of my past lives, I worked for the government—both as a federal employee and as a contractor in high-security organizations. The security briefings on those first days were powerful. I remember them, even ten years later. I remember the expectations they set, the threats they highlighted, the impact if realized, and what my role was in supporting the security mission and also how I might be targeted. It was personal, from day one.

Not all companies put security up front in the orientation process, however. The lack of messaging was noticeable to me for obvious reasons, but it's rarely missed by those outside of the security world. It just wasn't top of mind.

The orientation process is a unique opportunity to communicate what is important to the business, and important for the employee to remember. This is the ideal time to train developers in how to code securely, what the security standards are, and so on *before* they touch the code.

A secure coding boot camp (whether for a few days or a week), a program that includes interactive mentorship and real-world examples, will pay dividends down the road. Got developers in the seat already? Send them too. Many companies have budget and expectations for continuous learning for their employees. Some even require a number of hours of training a year as part of their performance measurement. In a skill-up year, you might be able to negotiate classes for cohorts of existing employees to go to the security engineering bootcamps. You could even incorporate this into a security champion program where developers are nominated by their management to attend—and most importantly, allocated time to do so. This practice of nomination, combined with some support from HR, can shift a developer's reaction from "I have to do this" to "I get to do this," with a developer viewing the designation of a security champion be one of prestige and not burden.

Getting Buy-In to Build

Even when folks know what to do and why, you will still run into the "so-what" response. Every team has to compete for time and resources in order to bring their new ideas to fruition—building a security-by-design capability is no different. As a security leader, you'll have to sell the merits of your secure development program and demonstrate why it's worthy of immediate and sustained buy-in, time, and budget. Here's where the art of storytelling coupled with all of that relationship building kicks in.

Make It Relatable, Make It Important, and Back It with Data

You might be surprised how many decision-makers get their security news from headlines in mainstream media and publications. You might also be surprised how many folks believe that their app or their practice could not be a target. "Our app doesn't have any PII or money flowing through it. What's the risk?" they say. If it touches other systems, it could be a valuable soft target for an attacker to leverage in order to get to a bigger target.

"Could this happen to us?" and "What could happen to us?" are questions you want to be ready and honored to answer. The art of storytelling in this sense involves contextualizing the what-ifs and the experience of others into something that is relatable to your environment.

Security conversations are expanding. Where they used to almost solely focus on data breaches, they've grown to include questions on more disruptive campaigns including ransomware or destructive attacks. With celebrity-level hacks and campaigns like the NotPetya destructive attacks (2017), the SolarWinds espionage campaign (2020), and the Colonial Pipeline ransomware incident (2021), organizations are becoming more aware of how what they develop and the technologies they use can be weaponized by attackers to not only compromise their company's assets, but also to affect their customers and the public.

In the case of NotPetya, for example, a trusted update from a small company's widely used tax software was compromised to infect a particular target in a destructive attack. The problem was that this update spread to all users, resulting in over $10B in collateral damage to unintended targets, including bringing shipping giant Maersk, which accounts for more than 20% of the world's shipping capacity, to a halt for days.

Using examples from headlines to tell the story of potential impact to your own organization and relating those examples to how your company develops products is only part of the storytelling process. You'll want to infuse those stories with data that can inform the value of what a security-by-design capability can bring and how it can be measured for success. We've already talked about the cost benefits of finding bugs up front in the development process versus afterwards. In general, companies spend more time and money finding and fixing flaws in postproduction than in the early development environment. According to IBM's System Science Institute, finding a flaw postproduction is six times more expensive than finding it preproduction, and fifteen times more expensive to fix in postproduction than in preproduction. NIST estimates that organizations can spend twenty-five times more on postproduction flaws.

Do some research and internal data gathering to translate industry trends for your organization. Odds are the data won't be in one place, so enlisting those relationships will be helpful in figuring out where to start. Like security, data to enable performance measurement can be an afterthought, and finding the right data can be difficult. Here are a few easier metrics to find that can help inform the scale of impact when translating industry trends:

- How many software defects and security flaws were found in the last year?
- How many defects were repeat findings?
- Have any defects led to incidents, outages, or compromises?

Once you have these numbers, you can help paint the picture of the potential benefit of shifting left with a security-by-design program. Next, you'll want to include planned metrics to measure program performance to the intended outcomes. It's important to note that creating and interpreting metrics is an entire discipline in itself and requires expertise. Enlist a data scientist to help you craft your story and support it with data so that what you're measuring can support the decisions and outcomes you're seeking. While many are enamored by the term data-driven decision-making, data rarely drives decisions alone when humans are involved. Data influences decisions; our experience and context play an equally important role.

The data scientist will help you determine what the data can and cannot be used for and help set expectations on baseline, cadence, and reasonableness for expected improvement. For example, if you're trying to show value of the program over time by measuring the decrease of repeated defects, your results are dependent on development cycle times. In other words, you'll only get one data point after each development cycle, so reporting cadence should correspond to when and how much data will be available to trend and analyze. If you have two-week sprints and want to measure repeated defects for each sprint after integrating a SAST tool, you'll want to have enough sprints pass to have statistically adequate data to show effects over time. You'll also need time to get a cohort through the training cycle to show the benefits of training in the overall solution.

Conclusion

Security by design involves fundamental changes across organizations and requires a culture shift in which safety becomes an integral part of the definition of quality and readiness. It's an investment in people, process, and technology that can result in a powerful competitive advantage. How we as security leaders communicate and develop the strategy for value and implementation is a key component in the achievement of a shift-left culture. Partnering with stakeholders to learn perspectives, share and scale skill sets, and co-create solutions is fundamental to success.

Notes

1. The OWASP Top 10 Web Application Security Vulnerabilities list (https://owasp.org/www-project-top-ten/) has been in place for many years. Many of the same vulnerabilities remain year after year.

2. Reports that publicly held companies file with the US Securities and Exchange Commission, available at SEC.gov

ANNE MARIE ZETTLEMOYER

Anne Marie Zettlemoyer is a senior security executive with over twenty years of experience in eight industries. Sitting at the intersection of business, security, and analytics, she has served as a trusted advisor for Fortune 500 companies, government agencies, law enforcement, security vendors, and think tanks.

Anne Marie is a Vice President of Security Engineering and Business Security Officer at Mastercard, is a visiting National Security Institute Fellow at GMU's Scalia Law School, and has held a number of strategic and technical security leadership roles, including Head of Security Architecture, Engineering and Solutions at Freddie Mac, Director of the Cyber Think Tank at Capital One, Director of Business Analytics at FireEye, and Special Advisor for the Director of the United States Secret Service.

Anne Marie has served on the board of directors and advisors for security companies and nonprofits as well as advocated for security policies and improvements on Capitol Hill. In addition to holding CISSP and CEH certifications, Anne Marie holds an MBA from the University of Michigan — Ann Arbor as well as undergraduate degrees in both accounting and finance.

9

From Enforcer to Strategic Partner
The Changing Role of Governance, Risk, and Compliance

BETH-ANNE BYGUM

TUCKED IN A WINDOW SEAT ON A SOUTHWEST AIRLINES flight, I started my familiar weekend route between Phoenix and Burbank. Opening my phone, I continued reading *The Pentagon's Brain*[1] by Annie Jacobsen. Surprisingly, Jacobsen's account of the birth and evolution of DARPA echoes the issues we face today as CISOs. Too often, we find ourselves faced with combating compromises in solutions that were designed from a place of trust versus security by design.

This theme comes up again in the Netflix original documentary *The Social Dilemma*.[2] I realized that we will continue to face this persistent problem if our focus on user experience design continues to outweigh security by design. Maintaining the critical balance between user experience and end-to-end data security is a fundamental design requirement.

The current emphasis on digital transformation and user experience is nothing new. Digital experiences are important, but the capabilities must be developed with security at the core for the services to be resilient and sustainable, at the same time maintaining the trust granted by our users and customers. Without this fundamental principle, organizations cannot fulfill their duty to ensure the confidentiality and integrity of information, systems, and data. As leaders, we perpetuate the problem unless we use methodologies that enforce the ability to design and configure security at the very core.

We could say this is the perfect storm created by the intersection of digital transformation, advanced computing platforms, increased connectivity between systems, and the ever-decreasing ability to pinpoint weaknesses that may result in a supply chain hack, infrastructure compromise, or significant data leakage. Upping the ante is the fact that the risk landscape is changing at an aggressive pace; a compliance executive must also accurately interpret concerns that undermine the confidentiality and integrity of data.

Compliance professionals and CISOs alike face a shift that originates from these direct and indirect drivers. It is reshaping our approach to define governance models, assess risk, implement right-size compliance requirements, and communicate residual risk to our leaders.

How can we deliver more value without overusing the bad-actor risk narrative? This chapter provides suggestions that may help you shift the governance and compliance role from enforcer to strategic enabler at your organization.

Information Governance Council: Oversight That Works

Compliance governing bodies often have a bad rap. Their work is perceived as overhead, processes that delay project timelines and create tasks that require lots of approvals. In too many cases the resulting guidance is redundant or, worse, may conflict between departments.

We can change the paradigm.

As organizations adopt advanced digital solutions and leverage the competitive advantage that next-generation computing offers, well-designed governance models accelerate innovation, expedite the adoption of new solutions, and can simplify the approval process.

Delays to timelines and the necessity for multiple approvals stem from disparate compliance tasks created using a departmental lens rather than an integrated risk review process lens. Historically, each compliance or risk team evaluates the use of data, regulatory requirements, security concerns, and the impact of technology separately from its own perspective.

Establishing an Information Governance Council offers a way to streamline approvals and guidance for new uses of technology and data. This approach seeks to bring all the relevant decision-makers into one group, with representation across departments.

Broad agreement from council members ensures that the organization's data compliance and information governance strategy contributes directly to corporate strategy. Depending upon your organization and industry, the naming convention of these areas may vary.

Compliance leaders should be part of the Information Governance Council. They may have titles like head of compliance, chief governance officer (CGO), or chief risk officer (CRO).

The council naturally includes employees representing the legal, privacy, information security, information systems, and technology product teams. It should also include representatives from Sourcing and Procurement to gain insight into investment road maps and minimize risks prior to purchase and throughout the contract management process. Adding such groups enables early detection of changes to the use of licensed data, systems, or information.

Your council's charter should be designed to:

- Streamline the evaluation of risk to your data or compliance posture, offering holistic and integrated guidance from the various stakeholders.

- Increase clarity about interpretation of requirements.

- Expedite approvals along the organization's integrated set of policies, standards, and practices. This creates efficiencies.

To be effective, the Information Governance Council must make decisions in a way that balances the concerns of the stakeholders.

One approach is to consciously adopt a decision-making model. Two categories of models for organizations are rational decision-making (for example, DECIDE[3]) and bounded decision-making; both can support organizational decision-making practices. Integrate the decision-making models with easy-to-follow financial, data treatment, and digital transformation thresholds. Adopting a decision-making model reduces approval cycles and streamlines existing processes. It also offers a concrete approach for vetting current and future data, compliance, and technology use cases.

Automating Compliance

Policymaking and compliance practices generally do not keep pace with technology changes. In addition to changes across the technical landscape, changes in regulations compound the need to understand expectations and translate them into requirements for system architects, developers, and engineers. The speed at which companies adopt cloud computing, digital technology, and advanced capabilities such as artificial intelligence is far surpassing the pace of our ability to adapt or evolve policies.

It is time to expedite the critical components of our practice and realize that technical interpretation of controls through automation is the best path forward.

Enabling automation will require some policy changes. Except for updates of recent data privacy regulations, most areas of compliance need a refresh to ensure that requirements can be implemented in code or configured in digital and automated solutions.

We need to lead by using the same leading-edge technology we are tasked to govern.

Traditional approaches to defining policy, monitoring compliance, and auditing adherence to requirements are under pressure. Current approaches are rigid and not easily automated.

Success in this area requires resisting the default approach: adding requirements to existing policy. Policies, like systems, require architecture and design review when new uses of data or new technologies are introduced. A fundamental rule is to avoid complexity and right-size compliance to meet regulatory expectations. This ensures systems are operating as intended to defend data.

We must revisit our approach to writing policy, keeping in mind the following:

- Understand the implications. We must understand current and next-generation technology, security, and audit capabilities prior to writing policies. The way we write policies can make things more difficult for systems and development teams because they are often translating policy requirements into code. Today we defend and govern using software that executes the intent of our policies and standards. Gone are the days when a risk or compliance program can be developed independently of understanding how a system or application will interpret and execute the intent of the control.

- Conduct a full review of policy and technical standards. Prioritize reviews of secure software development, solution delivery, vendor management, and defect management practices. Assess the level of awareness before attempting to introduce tech-relevant changes to policy. Update requirements associated with demonstrating control performance so that the automation of such tasks validates performance in a compliance assessment or audit.

- Adjust the periodic review and sampling process to evaluate the effectiveness and integrity of the code behind an automated rule. This code is the attestation you supply during an audit; it provides the appropriate level of assurance.

- Update the Information Governance Council's charter and the annual program to ensure that decisions and policy adjustments prepare for the introduction of next-generation technology and the use of data prior to the organization adopting the solutions. This will minimize implementation costs associated with delays or misunderstanding compliance requirements.

Making governance, risk, and compliance (GRC) technology-relevant streamlines decision-making and in some cases reduces the heat of discussions when transformational changes in architecture, code, or sharing data are introduced.

Training and Technology Briefings

As we discussed in the previous section, we are defending compliance practices related to code. If we do not understand the code and software that executes the requirements, how can we ensure the organization's ability to maintain the fundamentals of confidentiality, integrity, and assurance (CIA)?

If you've joined an organization or recently been appointed to lead the governance program, evaluate the level of technology awareness of those in the Information Governance Council. A series of technology briefings and training sessions may be needed to help council members become current in important areas. It is paramount that compliance professionals who support the CISO and enterprise risk teams keep up with techniques to automate compliance and in turn help educate everyone involved.

What does this mean to the compliance professional? Close the technical knowledge gaps by consistently putting time and effort into learning. For example:

- Have monthly training sessions given by your internal engineering and developer teams.

- Attend conferences where participants share how solutions are being used to perform security, compliance, and audit functions. Go to sessions with other compliance professionals or partner with other organizations to develop case studies or write white papers.

In technology briefings by the information systems or technology teams, ask them to highlight how the automation of controls will be configured to ensure confidentiality, integrity, and resilience.

If we don't transform the skills of information governance practitioners, we will encounter unintended residual risks. For example, we may not be able to spot security and compliance risks in software, automated in code, or outlined in contract terms. We may not notice a lack of adherence to policy because we are unable to detect the gap in the software.

Leaders are accountable to upskill and prepare assurance, risk, and compliance teams.

Becoming Purpose-Driven

All aspects of governance should be purpose-driven and technically informed.

A purpose-driven Information Governance Council addresses the limitations of traditional organizational or political boundaries in its charter. In addition to the topics listed previously, here are some other elements you may want to incorporate in your council's charter:

- Defined approaches to support increased adoption of automation and open-source code
- Clear expectations for the treatment of data using secure-by-design practices in both commercial applications and applications developed in-house
- Methods for incorporating up-to-date technology trends relevant to your industry so results maintain the required compliance posture

Sourcing and Contract Templates

Sourcing and contract templates are an upstream category of governance that may be overlooked in a traditional compliance governance model.

Inserting clearly defined terms and requirements into contract templates is a basic component of good contract management practices. This practice minimizes confusion and defines compliance expectations related to data processing, data treatment, and security transferred to the supplier or strategic partner.

Standard contract terms such as "reasonable and appropriate security controls" are no longer suitable. Such language does not convey specific technical expectations for the protection of information and data in the contract. This type of language may leave a company exposed given changes in technology as compared to the threat landscape.

Ensure that policies remain up to date and in force by sending out updated agreements automatically. Here are some contract terms to consider:

- Proactively define compliance requirements that should be automated across vendor systems or practices.

- Require compensating practices if full automation is not possible.

- Audit critical controls of connected third parties or strategic partners if automation is not possible.

- Consider how frequently contract templates should be updated to keep pace with increasing risks associated with changes in technology.

- Provide technology and compliance briefs to smaller strategic partners that may not have the resources to remain current with trends.

Earlier in this chapter, I acknowledged that our field has not always kept pace with the rapid acceleration of technology, advanced computing, and the expanding threat landscape. Staying up to date is even more important as we see increased attacks where threat actors are leveraging poor code, misconfiguration, or vulnerabilities not identified during patching, change control, or periodic reviews. The Information Governance Council and the governance lead have a more prominent role now in addressing these concerns in partnership with the head of architecture and cyber defense. Statistics show that revised proactive technology-informed policies simplify compliant practices, address gaps, and accelerate fast adoption.

Delivering Value in a Changing Environment

Global data privacy regulations continue to adjust, which is partly a reflection of changes across the threat landscape. It also reflects reduced tolerance for errors or mistakes that originate from basic noncompliant practices. An example is seen in recent regulations passed in California. Ten months after the California Consumer Privacy Act[4] (CCPA) came into effect, the State of California passed another law that amends it: the California Privacy Rights Act[5]

(CPRA), further strengthening regulatory expectations.

The new regulations along with economic pressures generated by a prolonged pandemic provide a unique opportunity for governance, risk, and compliance leaders in any organization to adjust strategy and deliver more value.

In times like these, management needs revised policy and clear directives that ensure compliance while enabling continued innovation. Even slight adjustments in strategy create additional value.

Here are a few concrete examples:

- Increase and enable automation. Put in place industry frameworks (as described later in this chapter) in a manner that enables automation to be easily adopted; results make it easier to identify policy gaps across the organization and systems.

- Add compensating controls such as analytic-based detection tools designed to alert when processes or systems deviate from policy.

- Accelerate the adoption of policy by communicating clear expectations using the same terms your information systems, information technology, and product teams use. Leaving the interpretation of policy requirements to others creates a delay in adopting and implementing the practice.

- Expand metrics and measures to highlight compliance challenges that could be addressed through technology investments.

Quantify Costs—No, Strike That—Quantify Value

Security and compliance professionals know how to calculate the fully loaded expense of operating a compliance and assurance function. However, we should not stop there. Aligning technology and compliance metrics and reporting dashboard strategies create an opportunity to convey traditional assurance practices in terms of business value and contribution. Compliance-related metrics, demonstrating adherence to requirements and regulations, encompass several areas. Examples include metrics associated with:

- Adherence to policies and requirements

- Metrics and indicators that show where the organization is falling out of compliance

- Costs associated with potential fines

Performance measures that demonstrate value to leadership include your service's contribution to reducing enterprise risks. Create visibility for leaders by integrating operating costs (such as the expense to process the various types of assessments and assurance audits) into the technology road map, current compliance posture, and risk reduction metrics.

Here are a few concrete examples:

- Develop a dashboard to track the relationship between system life cycle upgrade or decommission projects and the reduction of residual compliance risks (such as security exposure, regulatory fines, and compliance-related findings).

- Calculate the increased transference of risk as connected strategic vendors and partners carry cyber liability coverage.

Operational metrics are another area where the compliance lead can transform performance and demonstrate value. Here are a few questions to review for your organization:

- Does an assessment require two or three security and compliance professionals to complete? For example, is a senior security engineer required to complete the technical portion of an assessment while a GRC professional completes the policy review?

- How is your organization structured? Do you have an overdesigned service model where tasks pass multiple times back and forth between team members?

- How many assessment forms or types does your team process?

- Are you leveraging training designed to increase cross-team technical and policy skills?

- Is your team training goal designed to reduce the number of resources required to complete security assessments?

- How many assessments is your organization processing per year? Do you annually break down the cost per assessment? Do you measure how many times an assessment requires multiple resources to process?

In my experience of working with firms that provide outsourced security assessments and independent third-party audit/attestation solutions, costs range from $5K to $15K for the former and $150K to $350K+ for the latter. The average cost to complete an assessment by an internal compliance department ranges from $450 to $1,000 per assessment depending upon complexity. Combined average hourly wages of professionals and the number of hours needed to complete an assessment further increase operating costs.

Incorporate these numbers into your team's value determination.

The traditional approach of segmenting tasks—the review for completing technical risk assessments, third-party/vendor risk assessments, contract reviews, and security assurance reviews—requires resources with similar skill sets. Completion of these tasks increases your operating costs.

I share these thoughts from experience. There were times when I reviewed budgets and noted the number of resources required to assess risk. I asked myself why we require two or three resources to determine risk. If we defend at the level of code, we should assess risk at the same level. It was at that point that I realized that I could operate a more effective and cost-efficient team if the technical skills across the organization were balanced. The result was a reduction of duplication in the Information Governance Council operations, creating value and cost savings.

This is an example of a process improvement exercise that can identify operational efficiency gains and potential areas for adding value to the organization.

The increased reliance on seamless technology and the approach to ensure compliance via digital solutions mean that the heads of architecture, engineering, IT, and compliance must also align their road maps to these compliance metrics.

Such alignment increases early detection of issues before the organization becomes noncompliant. These actions create increased value and reduce overall costs associated with enterprise compliance risks. Be sure to quantify such savings and demonstrate how an integrated approach to compliance creates value and saves money at the same time.

TYPES OF FRAMEWORKS

Frank Kim of the SANS Institute categorizes frameworks as control frameworks, program frameworks, and risk frameworks.[6]

Control frameworks measure the state of technical capabilities and the maturity of security in the organization. If your organization is defining its first set of security and compliance controls, you may want to implement NIST 800-53 and CIS Controls (CSC). These frameworks assist in:

- Defining a baseline set of controls
- Assessing the state of technical capabilities
- Prioritizing the implementation of controls
- Developing an initial road map for the security team

Program frameworks such as ISO 27001 and NIST CSF[7] measure the management of the overarching program. These frameworks assist in defining:

- The state of the overall security program
- The structure for a comprehensive security program
- An approach for measuring the maturity and conducting industry comparisons
- A simplified communication with business leaders

Risk frameworks such as NIST 800-39, 800-37, 800-30; ISO 27005; and FAIR[8] help assess, measure, and prioritize risks to the organization. These frameworks assist in showing you how to:

- Define key process steps for assessing and managing risk
- Structure the risk management program
- Identify, measure, and quantify risk
- Prioritize security activities

For more details, watch Kim's full presentation from RSA.[9]

Evolve Your Use of Maturity Frameworks

A standard practice across compliance organizations is measuring the posture and compliance efforts using industry-recognized maturity frameworks. It is a convenient and vetted approach to demonstrate the strength of a compliance program. Examples of widely acknowledged frameworks include:

- Healthcare Insurance Portability and Accountability Act (HIPAA)
- Payment Card Industry's Data Security Standard (PCI DSS)
- National Institute of Standards and Technology (NIST) SP 800-53
- National Institute of Standards Cybersecurity Framework
- International Organization of Standardization (ISO) 27000 Series

These models provide means of conveying best practices for cyber defense, controls to measure risk, and terms to convey technical concerns in a manner that aligns with management strategy, enterprise risk, and expectations outlined by the board of directors. Based on the organization's security program and strategy, the CISO and the head of governance determine the balance of frameworks, controls, and performance metrics needed to reflect the compliance posture and security readiness of the organization.

Metrics and Measures

Metrics and measures must also evolve. In addition to relying on industry frameworks, organizations should create appropriate compliance hygiene metrics to determine if operational metrics comply with policy. Metrics are foundational to enabling a secure-by-design culture. They promote a cyclical dynamic where we adjust performance indicators and ensure that executives monitor sustained practices.

Maturity and Hygiene Metrics

The Information Governance Council requires a blend of maturity and hygiene metrics to monitor the compliance posture and security practices across the organization. Because maturity metrics are an indication of how advanced a program and practice are at an organization, hygiene metrics determine how actively adopted security practices are within critical operations. Examples of insightful hygiene metrics include:

- Rigor associated with periodic review of critical practices (for example, user and privilege access review, password management, firewall rules, connected entities, and so on)

- Vulnerability management—Number of noncompliant assets and the length of age

- Application scanning and defect management—Remediation before deploying to production

- Configuration of key security controls—Encryption standards, cloud security, APIs

Once the balance of frameworks and hygiene controls are defined, an integrated dashboard gives management visibility into the state of technical risks, the potential exposure of the organization's security posture, and the evolution of the program.

Metric Control Plan

Whether you subscribe to the belief that we are in the fourth generation of the electronic age or at the beginning of the experience age, as GRC professionals we are tasked with balancing governance in a manner that enables next-generation computing and future technology while reducing unseen risks that can undermine an organization's compliance posture. We have to forecast environmental, data, and social compliance issues that may not yet be understood.

We saw this with the COVID-19 pandemic. To continue working, people and organizations adopted revised business models and new approaches to deliver needed services and products. Organizations that successfully navigate such twists and turns do so by tapping into insights formed by reaching into uncharted areas of available data, trends, and operational metrics.

A metric control plan defines the method by which an organization maintains the integrity of controls. It defines measures to determine if controls are operating as intended and methods to track key performance risk indicators. These measures support specific areas of maturity and annual goals that advance organizational hygiene practices.

The Information Governance Council is an enabler of working from a metric control plan. It starts with a clear, purposefully defined set of key performance indicators and accompanying metrics. The metrics are an organization's compliance baseline. The Information Governance Council also generates insights that support the transition to next-generation solutions. The metric control plan is the engine that connects policy, frequency of periodic control reviews, and measured results, all of which propel the organization. Measuring conformance and alignment to a defined risk posture produces insights. These insights propel your innovation strategy through increased efficiency or transformations that enable revenue and growth.

This model supports evolving the metric control plan but also serves as justification for a comprehensive GRC solution if your team is still managing the journey via spreadsheets. The power of a metric control plan is realized once the key performance indicators, control framework, and other environmental drivers are implemented in an automated control monitoring tool. As we discussed earlier in this chapter, we are at a juncture where compliance professionals must understand and harness the power of automation and technology. Automated GRC tools enable faster detection of areas trending toward noncompliance or potential fines. Integrating advanced technology, such as artificial intelligence and machine learning, to accelerate the identification of themes proactively identifies high-risk issues that could impact business performance.

Conclude with a Culture of Compliance

This may be the last section of this chapter, but it is the first step in cultivating dynamic change. Governance becomes a business enabler when the security, compliance, and privacy-by-design mindset is embedded in the culture. The shift is sustained when measurements are defined with specific, tangible, and achievable targets.

Ways to operationalize the shift:

- Frequent technology briefings not only inform the Information Governance Council but also spur blue sky thinking across perspectives of this diverse group. It will uncover an approach to writing policy that enables versus restricts the organization.

- Use cross-lens focus and working groups to validate and enable the integrated guidance that your team created.

- Integrate the company's decision-making, problem solving, and performance targets into your compensation system. The shift supports a dynamic culture of compliance.

Here are some examples of processes that, when incentivized, reward employees for sustaining a culture of compliance:

- Adapt problem solving in a manner that results in improved secure-by-design practices.
- Vet scenarios using the defined compliance-by-design principles and demonstrate results to management.
- Establish practices designed to morph as technology evolves.
- Write policies in a manner that enables rapid but secure application development and technology adoption.
- Foster policies designed to accelerate forward momentum and new uses of data.

As a long-time practitioner in the GRC field, I welcome the transformation from governance as enforcer to governance as enabler.

This is your chance to embrace the shift and advance as a more strategic partner. You have the opportunity to catapult growth, technology, innovation, and exploratory programs while you advance security and improve the organization's compliance posture. Your refreshed program will create direct business value—revenue—in addition to improving traditional risk reduction metrics. With a cross-team and cross-practice lens, you are better positioned to help organizations you serve face challenges and realize opportunities as they adopt new uses of data while implementing digital technology targets.

Notes

1. https://www.littlebrown.com/titles/annie-jacobsen/the-pentagons-brain/9780316371650/
2. https://www.imdb.com/title/tt11464826/
3. https://www.flightliteracy.com/the-decision-making-process-the-decide-model/
4. https://oag.ca.gov/privacy/ccpa
5. https://privacyrights.org/resources/california-privacy-rights-act-overview
6. https://www.frankkim.net/blog/how-to-make-sense-of-cybersecurity-frameworks
7. https://www.nist.gov/cyberframework/online-learning/components-framework
8. https://www.risklens.com/resource-center/blog/the-fair-model-in-90-seconds
9. https://youtu.be/dt2IqidgpS4

BETH-ANNE BYGUM

Enjoying a circuitous route through a number of information systems, security, and compliance roles, Beth-Anne Bygum leverages her approach to connect individuals and galvanize change. As the Chief Security & Compliance Officer for Acxiom, Beth-Anne is responsible for all aspects of the global cybersecurity strategy, enterprise risk management program, and information governance. Collaborating with leaders across the company, she advances innovative solutions to enable digital and cloud transformation strategies.

Beth-Anne has worked in the consumer products goods, biotechnology, and technology sectors. The advice provided in this chapter summarizes twenty-five years of experience directing portfolios and programs related to information security, risk management, IT compliance, information governance, and IT training.

10

Don't Let Cyber Supply Chain Security Be Your Weakest Link

TERRY ROBERTS

N THE DIGITAL AGE, SUPPLY CHAIN RISK DUE TO THE SIGNIFICANT use of information and operational technology vendors and service contractors has dramatically expanded the threat landscape for all businesses and organizations, making the protection of their reputation and revenue far more complex. Today we call this cyber supply chain risk management, or C-SCRM—a much-needed discipline, practice, and body of knowledge, of ever-increasing focus and emphasis in our interconnected world. C-SCRM is challenging for even top security and risk managers not to mention executive teams and boards of directors.

What Does C-SCRM Encompass?

In exploring C-SCRM, let's start with the NIST definition:[1]

> "Cyber Supply Chain Risk Management (C-SCRM) is the process of identifying, assessing, and mitigating the risks associated with the distributed and interconnected nature of IT/OT product and service supply chains. It covers the entire life cycle of a system (including design, development, distribution, deployment, acquisition, maintenance, and destruction) as supply chain threats and vulnerabilities may intentionally or unintentionally compromise an IT/OT product or service at any stage."

That is a very detailed definition. Let's break it down bit by bit.

What does "cyber supply chain risk management" mean? In this context, cyber means everything that is interconnected; all information technology and operational technology (IT/OT) hardware, software, and services including platforms, devices, architectures, applications, online services, communications, and datasets. And while C-SCRM does not include elements of the traditional supply chain like raw ingredients for food or fabric for clothing, it does encompass "smart" elements of those supply chains, such as smart tags used for inventory and tracking of pallets or expensive individual items.

What is cyber supply chain management? It is "the process of identifying, assessing, and mitigating the risks associated with the distributed and interconnected nature of IT/OT product and service supply chains." This part of the definition takes into its scope most IT systems, whether on-premises, cloud-based, or mobile, as well as anything with embedded software, like a fleet of cars or medical equipment.

Cyber supply chain risk management "covers the entire life cycle of a system (including design, development, distribution, deployment, acquisition, maintenance, and destruction)." From this portion of the definition alone, you can see that C-SCRM activities cross departments and functions, spanning organizational silos.

The final part of the NIST definition explains why this comprehensive approach is important because "supply chain threats and vulnerabilities may intentionally or unintentionally compromise an IT/OT product or service at any stage." The risk is pervasive and crosses business and mission operations because of our significant reliance on IT/OT systems.

Although broad, this definition will keep us focused on one of the arenas of today's supply chains that is rapidly evolving and increasing in complexity.

Our cyber supply chain is now as critical to us as our food chain. It is integral to our overall environment and impacts our entire ecosystem with its work, social, and economic interplay and dependencies.

The Ultimate Moving Target

If you love solving high-impact, complex problems using innovative frameworks, technologies, and analytics, C-SCRM is a great professional field to work in.

What is more important than identifying, prioritizing, and mitigating digital age risks from impacting your company, organization, or customers? The relentless pace of advances in technology and in the development of software tools and applications, the ongoing changes and fragility in the rapidly globalizing supply chain, and the global and evolving threats all add to the complexity and impact.

Establishing a risk baseline and continuously keeping up with the breadth of what is involved—what you have, who built it, what it is connected to, how it is used, how it could be subverted, and how it must be protected, defended, and responded to—is foundational. It is a significant undertaking that requires executive-level focus, hands-on management, and accountability. C-SCRM also demands repeatable frameworks and scalable processes, knowledge of the ecosystem, and technical and business acumen.

Of course, since this ecosystem moves at the speed of technology, this knowledge base must be continually reviewed, refreshed, and refined as the vendor solution and service base, the operating environment, and the threat actors, vectors, and intentions continue to change.

C-SCRM is not limited to hardware and software resilience and assurance. The executive and management levels must also assess risks that result from their business and mission functions; reliance on and connections with their partners, teammates, vendors, and suppliers; and the processes and people who implement and manage them, only a portion of which is under their aegis or control.

The world economy has become very specialized and fragmented, further complicating our supply chains. The norm is for a small business to have more than twenty suppliers and for a large manufacturer to have thousands. Consequently, the activities of CSOs, CIOs, and CISOs necessarily include vetting, selecting, contracting, and integrating a myriad of product lines and service vendors with their own supply chains, linkages, and dependencies, thereby compounding the risks.

And, lest we forget, it is called risk management because it is impossible to provide complete assurance against every possible threat, so we must consider which practical, prioritized actions can and should be taken to address the most damaging and probable of risks to the organization's crown jewels, within resource and business constraints.

C-SCRM CHALLENGES

- Scope – A global interconnected and ever-expanding IT/OT supply chain.

- Sector Governance, Compliance, and Audit – IT/OT regulatory frameworks are additive.

- Many Solutions and Vetting of Vendors – Many solutions and the ongoing need to vet them and their risks.

- Secure Code/Software Assurance – 90% of all vulnerabilities result from software weaknesses.

- Tech Advances Like IoT/Cloud/5G – Each bringing a new set of risks.

- Software Functionality and Development – New business and mission apps every day.

- Scaling Talent, Training, and Education – Millions more people needed.

- Management and Contracting for Services – Established contractors typically choose repeatable processes and familiar technology over innovation.

- Myriad Technology Solutions to Consider – Continuous vetting, testing, integrating.

- Daunting Complexity – The sum total of all of these challenges.

The Expansion of Software-Based Functionality

Software, software, software: It is the foundational building block of the information and digital age. Software also changes the risk dynamic across digital devices, networks, architectures, and systems of systems. The dramatic growth of software-driven functionality is directly related to the ever-evolving breadth of business and mission apps and features.

Software as a percentage of the embedded functionality in all of our platforms such as planes, cars, unmanned aerial vehicles, appliances, and devices has grown exponentially. This trend has enabled dynamic product innovation and delivery of new features and capabilities faster than ever before. Many organizations become enamored of and addicted to new applications, solutions, and tools without sufficient concern for the increased attack surface and the inherent complexities of tracking a software-based global supply chain.

The software supply chain alone poses considerable and complex risks, detailed in a report by the Atlantic Council. As much as 90% of IT vulnerabilities derive from software weaknesses, according to Rich Pethia, the founder of the original Computer Emergency Response Team at Carnegie Mellon University.

Today everything from watches to cars to airplanes runs software, and everything that has software-based functionality can be hacked. With 5G and the increased use of edge processing, the attack surface expands dramatically.

Hardware Supply Chain Risks

While software empowers innovation and reduces time to market, it still runs on hardware that does not change as often and that involves different components, vendors, and supply chains. As noted in the 2017 Report of the Defense Science Board Task Force on Cyber Supply Chain, "The supply chain for microelectronics parts is complex, involving multiple industry sectors. Each sector sells to each of the others."[2] The report refers to "risk from the malicious insertion of defects of malware into microelectronics and embedded software, and from the exploitation of latent vulnerabilities in these systems."

NOTPETYA: A $10B CAUTIONARY TALE

NotPetya was a worm delivered in an update to tax preparation software used in Ukraine. The worm quickly spread around the globe, rendering infected computers worthless and wiping them clean. NotPetya infected vast numbers of machines, disrupting operations for multinational corporations such as Maersk, FedEx, and Merck & Co., resulting in over $10 billion in damages and making it one of the costliest cyberattacks in history. (Find out more about NotPetya from Wired[3] or Vice.[4])

Some of the most egregious incidents are based upon threat vectors coming from state-sponsored cyber actors who are often motivated by industrial espionage, money, political disruption, or all three. Christopher Wray, director of the FBI, gave a summer 2020 speech at the Hudson Institute where he lays out the many dimensions of cyber threats from one nation-state and their real-world consequences.[5]

The threat is real, it has no boundaries, it has cost the United States billions of dollars already, and it is getting worse each year.

THE SOLARWINDS SUPPLY CHAIN COMPROMISE

SolarWinds, like NotPetya, involved weaponized software updates. Its impact is massive and still being assessed. CISA has created a supply chain compromise[6] web page dedicated to tracking the latest implications of this attack. This web page links to authoritative press releases, emergency directives, and alerts and guidance. In part, the page is generically named because the SolarWinds attack has implications for commonly used business environments such as Microsoft Azure and Microsoft 365.

A comprehensive approach to C-SCRM involves people, process, and technology. We will touch on all three areas.

People: It Takes a Village

The fact that supply chain risk management is challenging doesn't mean it is impossible. Security and technology leaders, including CSOs, CIOs, and CISOs, must prioritize and move forward.

Let's start with the key area of people—specifically, getting the right people in place to tackle the challenges. Understanding the breadth of the environment is foundational. This demands knowledgeable leadership and technical and operational expertise.

Getting the right leaders focused on the problem is an essential first step and can be helpful in signaling commitment to addressing the issues, which helps bring in people with the types of expertise required.

When thinking through how to organize teams, it is useful to consider agile development constructs where teams include experts from across the life cycle—design, development, test, and operations. Similarly, the supply chain risk management teams need to be able to look at everything from design, acquisition, test, and operations (including knowledge of the threats), all the way through destruction.

Automation is rapidly becoming critical to success in this area. As noted, understanding the environment—the vendors, products, components, issues, versions, patches, connections, and threats—is foundational. Yet even for knowledgeable personnel, it rapidly becomes impossible to keep track of all of the microelectronics, software components, and versions in a very large environment. These reviews and assessments must essentially be continuous as the environments continue to evolve. Data collection, tracking, and record keeping must be automated. And as new tools become available, they should be employed to highlight areas for risk mitigation and further research.

Because so many capabilities in large environments are contracted, either as components or services, it is also important for CISOs to carefully review their contracting language and constructs. Areas demanding particular focus include data rights, flow-downs, reporting, and incentive alignment. Ensuring that contractor incentives are aligned with those of the contracting organization is both key and nontrivial and often requires more technical knowledge and precision in language and terminology than might be considered normal when acquiring a product or service. However, too many things can go awry if the incentives aren't aligned, starting with things as simple as flow-down to subcontractors and reporting (for example, what must be reported, and when and how). Another area requiring attention is data rights—what data will you need from your vendor in order to manage risk across your supply chain?

Process: It Takes a Framework

Given the complexity and breadth of areas involved in C-SCRM, it is helpful to use a published framework as a point of reference and a benchmark to see how you are doing.

Many of the C-SCRM frameworks draw from and build on one another. You may be mandated to use a particular framework, but even if you are not, consider using one to inform your efforts and communicate with your partners.

Traditional IT SCRM Approaches

How has IT supply chain management been handled in the past from a process standpoint? What can we learn from those practices?

Traditional approaches combined supply chain management and risk management, both of which are management processes with roots in logistics, in manufacturing, and, after World War II, in operations research. Manufacturers refined their supply chain management processes to support just-in-time inventory with its attendant bottom-line benefits, while also minimizing risk. The focus was on ensuring products were available when they were needed.

As systems became more complex, and with increasing dependence on software-driven functionality as an ever-growing percentage of capabilities, organizations began to update these processes to accommodate IT-based programs built on and around what are now traditional waterfall system development models, typically with people performing audit and compliance checks.

NIST and ISO

That was just the beginning. Since then a number of C-SCRM frameworks, practices, and regulations have been created, vetted, and established, including notably NIST SP 800-171, which is the comprehensive framework used by sophisticated federal contractors, as well as ISO standards, including ISO 28000[10] and ISO 20243.[11]

Frameworks have been part of C-SCRM from the beginning. C-SCRM emerged in 2008 as part of the Comprehensive National Cybersecurity Initiative (CNCI). I played a small role as a key stakeholder for the US Department of the Navy, with the leader of it all, then Director of National Intelligence Mike McConnell and his executive lead Melissa Hathaway. One of CNCI's areas of focus was to "develop a multi-pronged approach for global supply chain risk management."

In 2009, NIST co-led CNCI 11 Working Group 2, Life Cycle Processes and Standards, with the Department of Defense. That working group's tasks included "developing supply chain tools, resources and risk management practices, in partnership with industry."

CMMC as a Framework

CMMC is a 2020 regulatory mandate for defense contractors. It includes five maturity levels, making varying degrees of certification achievable. But with the lack of systemic enablement, especially for companies without CIOs and CISOs, CMMC has been criticized as having an unrealistic timeline for compliance.

Because CMMC is a new framework and therefore the least familiar, we cover it in a bit more detail.

CMMC can be a useful framework for businesses of any size seeking to create a repeatable and holistic C-SCRM program because CMMC offers levels of compliance (not a more binary compliant or noncompliant approach). Shown in Figure 10-1, the levels outline an incremental approach for improving cybersecurity. Level 1 addresses the requirements for basic cyber hygiene.

CMMC Levels

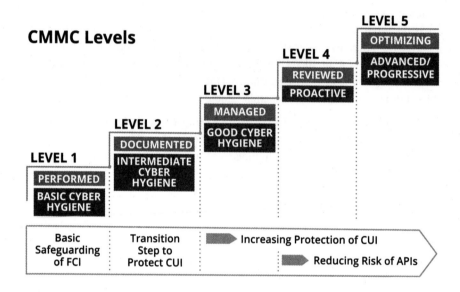

Figure 10-1. Levels in CMMC offer an incremental approach to compliance

The five CMMC levels are made up of seventeen cybersecurity domains, as shown in Figure 10-2. Each CMMC control is categorized into one of these seventeen domains; this figure lists the abbreviations for easy reference.

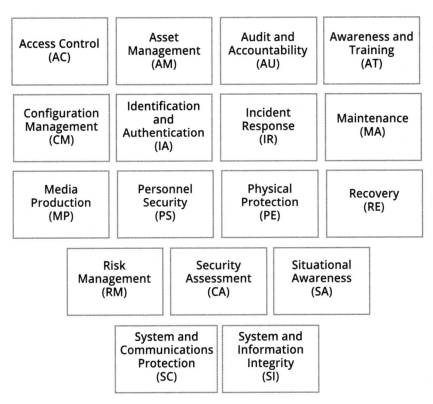

Figure 10-2. Cybersecurity domains and their abbreviations

CMMC builds on domains from existing frameworks. For example, fourteen of the seventeen cybersecurity domains in Figure 10-2 come from the security-related areas in Federal Information Processing Standards (FIPS) publication 200 and the security requirement families from NIST 800-171. The remaining three security domains (asset management [AM], recovery [RE], and situational awareness [SA]) are drawn primarily from the following frameworks:

- FAR 52.204-21
- NIST 800-53 rev 4
- NIST 800-171 rev2
- NIST 800-171B
- NIST Cybersecurity Framework
- CMU SEI CERT Resilience Management Model (RMM)
- International Organization for Standardization (ISO) 27002:2013
- Center for Internet Security (CIS) Critical Security Controls (CSC) 7.1

NIST 800-171 Compliance and CMMC Audits Are Not the Same

It's important to understand that completing a CMMC audit and eventually being CMMC certified at a specific level (from 1 through 5) does not equate to your organization being compliant with NIST 800-171.

While NIST 800-171 focuses primarily on the 110 controlled unclassified information (CUI) controls, it also requires compliance with an additional sixty-three Non-Federal Organization (NFO) controls. Therefore, to comply with NIST SP 800-171, your organization needs to comply with both CUI and NFO controls.

A Living Risk Framework

Cyber supply chain risk spans the entire life cycle of a system, from design to operations right up through destruction. While activities can be segmented, assessing and adequately addressing the risks requires more than a narrow view focused on specific components or technologies.

Risk management, particularly for high-consequence systems, requires visibility not only across the system life cycle, but also visibility and access to information about the operating environment and to current information about each of the components. This is no small task.

And, because the information environment is constantly evolving and in many cases so are the systems and architectures themselves, supply chain risk management requires a living risk framework that is in continuous risk discovery, prioritization, and mitigation mode—making it a task that is never really done.

Technology: It Takes Automation

In the past, we've relied on primarily manual audits and even on self-attestation, where vendors and partners submit information to certify their own security practices.

With today's technology, such traditional approaches are at best outmoded. They don't scale, don't use all publicly available global risk datasets, and don't integrate with AI-assisted C-SCRM algorithms and analytics.

Modern approaches to C-SCRM use software platforms that incorporate automation, AI, and machine learning. Because the challenges are myriad and multidimensional, it makes sense to enlist computers to help us tackle these challenges.

In essence, we could say it takes an army—meaning an army of computers, modern digital solutions that analyze more data than any human can.

It is time to start looking at solutions that provide a baseline of what is discoverable and knowable. Such solutions can map the baseline to risk frameworks and rate each supplier or vendor accordingly. They may offer an interactive dashboard of knowledge, alerting, and real-time action and risk mitigation engagement. This can become the new C-SCRM baseline, an approach that is much more powerful, enabling, and practical in the digital age.

Innovation and Automation Beat Compliance Perfection

For decades comprehensive frameworks with controls that are primarily audit and compliance focused have ruled. As many know, audit and compliance checklists are foundational but not by themselves sufficient, especially against the current threat landscape.

Over the past five years, those involved in cyber risk and assurance research and development have created solutions to help organizations gain risk visibility across silos. I have vetted more than a thousand such solutions with my team and have seen dramatic advancement in capabilities that are scalable and affordable.

This begs another question: How do we "cross the chasm" from primarily manpower-intensive audit and compliance best practices and tools to next-generation risk management technology solutions and automated practices?

My basic formula has three steps:

1. Conduct a resource baseline for C-SCRM. List your critical processes and determine what you are spending on personnel, tools, and resources for each of them.

2. Be open to cutting-edge analytics, automation, collaboration, and documentation platforms and technologies. Work with partners to vet and assess capabilities with efficiency and effectiveness, with a focus on meeting your key business and mission objectives.

3. Stop "throwing people" at new C-SCRM regulations, requirements, and scalability challenges. Take the time to vet and put in place smart tech. This is the only way to save resources and keep up with both compliance and risk, thereby allowing your team to focus on what humans do best: risk mitigation and accountability.

A Footnote on Cyber Research and Development

I've had the honor of managing diverse scientific and technical teams across government, industry, and academia since the late 1990s. I have become convinced that our body of knowledge in IT resilience, software assurance, and cybersecurity is woefully sparse compared with centuries of knowledge of the physical sciences. With our global dependency on IT systems, architectures, devices, apps, and communications and the magnitude and breadth of threats all evolving in real time as software is continuously developed and launched, it is time to prioritize cyber and software research and development.

Cyber-focused scientific research, development, and innovation requires additional government and industry resources, focus, collaboration, and documentation as well as continuous testing and advancement. We need an open research and development road map that shows what is taking place where so that we are sharing key results and collaborating to identify key gaps in understanding and capability. In addition, I would say that the United States is not effectively focused on the continuous creation, vetting, and adoption of innovative cyber solutions and best practices to address pressing cyber risk and resilience challenges.

Features to Look for in a Modern C-SCRM Solution

A modern C-SCRM solution should incorporate:

- A comprehensive approach to accessing and leveraging publicly available risk datasets

- Risk-based AI and machine learning features to advance analytics

- APIs for seamless integration and continuous improvement

- Integrated C-SCRM documentation and engagement SaaS dashboard

Continuous Risk Monitoring with Open Datasets

Risk discovery, prioritization, and alerting are imperative to the identification and management of today's IT risks in near-real time. The amount of publicly available risk data has grown dramatically over the past decade whether from open media, publications, subscriptions, assessments, or social media and web scraping. This breadth of open risk data, combined with AI-based risk tradecraft analytics, provides a critical baseline of globally discoverable, prioritized risk indicators and alerts that can then be documented and acted upon by the C-SCRM team.

For example, by fully leveraging and mapping publicly available sources to proven cyber and business risk frameworks, the following risk insights can be gained and updated continuously:

- Who are the company's suppliers, where are their production locations, and have their suppliers had recent financial or operational issues?

- Are foundational security practices in place and up to date, such as SSL certificates or patch management?

- Has the company or organization experienced any data breaches or botnet attacks over the past year or two?

As a cyber intelligence and global risk professional, I approach these risk analytics as an advanced, additional risk perspective—not to be dismissed.

Rather these risk indicators are important signs that are worth looking into. Bringing together such risk datasets forms a satellite image of risk, a unique and powerful independent perspective that should be carefully reviewed, weighed, and mitigated as appropriate. In the field of cyber intelligence, we see an outside-in or hacker view as critical to staying on top of your company's risk landscape as well as that of your suppliers.

AI-Based Risk Analytics and Functionality

In addition to many commercial solutions now fully leveraging publicly available datasets, the power of these risk analytics comes from developing AI algorithms that integrate cyber and supply chain risk and resilience principles and logic, enabling risk identification and prioritization at a speed never before attained. The advent of mature cyber risk controls that map to the NIST Framework, CIS Controls,[12] or CMMC provides a foundation for these AI algorithms that can evolve and advance the more they are used, which creates a machine learning dynamic over time.

AI algorithms move us closer to the holistic and continuous risk view required for an effective C-SCRM program. For example, software changes rapidly (in a matter of months), and hardware changes over a course of years; nonetheless software runs on hardware, and the two cannot be considered in isolation. This dichotomy is itself an oversimplification, as most applications have a software stack that includes a database, which has its own vulnerabilities.

APIs and Integration

When evaluating C-SCRM solutions, consider whether they are API-compatible with other solutions in your cybersecurity portfolio. The goal is a holistic view, and compatible APIs make that much easier, especially as various products evolve.

SaaS Versus On-Premises

Cloud-based software-as-a-service (SaaS) solutions offer a number of advantages. Consider software administration tasks like updates. Instead of keeping track of software updates, SaaS solutions are automatically updated as the vendor, who manages the software, rolls out new features and changes. Closely related is another important point of differentiation for emerging solutions: make sure that any solution you adopt is maintained by an in-house development team so that updates and fixes arrive in a timely fashion. If you choose an on-premises solution, you then take on the administration and maintenance of that platform. In our experience, platforms that require maintenance by an in-house team tend to get outdated, falling into disuse over time.

Another advantage of SaaS platforms is that you can have multiple administrators. In that way, each group can administer their own functional area. For example, the CIO team may focus on the cyber aspects of vendor risk, and the legal and CFO team can administer and configure the contractual and audit part of the platform. Having an integrated platform drives collaboration and enables synchronization of supply chain risk management.

Even with the best software solutions, however, there is still work to be done, as discussed next.

Change Management: It Comes Back to the Village

C-SCRM systems are helpful, but in practice, their adoption is challenging because it requires real change. Taking a holistic approach breaks down the silos in your organization, and that is often easier said than done. Adopting a C-SCRM solution requires adapting to that solution, and that means change, which is challenging for the entire team.

Some parts of the supply chain move at cyber speed and experience rapid changes and updates; other parts of the organization manage equipment with life spans measured in decades. Naturally each group requires a different approach to risk and change management.

For example, procurement experts are accustomed to particular processes, and innovative solutions will change and often advance those processes. Vendor management may still be done in spreadsheets (I wish I could say I hadn't seen that in the real world time and again).

The business process transition is the most difficult portion of adopting modern C-SCRM solutions. Adopting new platforms impacts all your silos and your current business processes. It takes time and effort to implement these changes from a business process and performance perspective.

Conclusion

C-SCRM encompasses a breadth of responsibility with many inherent challenges. As such it is perfect for an approach that combines people, process, and technology, informed by as much data as possible, to create an environment that protects intellectual property and sensitive data while empowering innovation.

Notes

1. https://www.nist.gov/risk-management

2. https://dsb.cto.mil/reports/2010s/DSBCyberSupplyChainExecutiveSummary-Distribution_A.pdf

3. https://www.wired.com/story/notpetya-cyberattack-ukraine-russia-code-crashed-the-world/

4. https://www.vice.com/en/article/7x5vnz/notpetya-ushered-in-a-new-era-of-malware

5. https://www.fbi.gov/news/speeches/the-threat-posed-by-the-chinese-government-and-the-chinese-communist-party-to-the-economic-and-national-security-of-the-united-states

6. https://www.cisa.gov/supply-chain-compromise

7. https://www.iso.org/standard/44641.html

8. https://www.iso.org/standard/74399.html

9. https://csrc.nist.gov/publications/detail/sp/800-171/rev-2/final

10. https://www.iso.org/standard/44641.html

11. https://www.iso.org/standard/74399.html

12. https://www.cisecurity.org/controls/

TERRY ROBERTS

Terry Roberts has established the first CyberSecurity Online Exchange—enabling all businesses (especially midsize and small companies) to have continuous online access to automated cyber risk profiles, scorecards, action plans, and affordable products, services, insights, and trends industrywide.

Previously, Terry was the VP for Cyber Engineering and Analytics at TASC, running cyber/IT, financial, and business analytics across innovative technical services. Prior to TASC, Terry was Executive Director of the Carnegie Mellon Software Engineering Institute, leading the technical body of work for the entire US Interagency, with a special focus on leveraging and transitioning commercial innovation and acquisition excellence to government programs and capabilities and establishing the Emerging Technologies Center and Cyber Intelligence Consortium.

Before transitioning to industry in 2009, Terry Roberts was the Deputy Director of Naval Intelligence (DDNI), where she led, together with the Director of Naval Intelligence, more than 20,000 intelligence and information-warfare military and civilian professionals and managed more than $5 billion in resources, technologies, and programs globally, leading the initial approach for the merging of Naval Communications and Intelligence under the OPNAV N2/N6 and the creation of the Information Dominance Corps.

An intelligence professional for over thirty years, Terry has held many senior intelligence positions, including Director of Intelligence, Commander Naval Forces Europe and Commander-in-Chief NATO AFSOUTH; Director, Defense Intelligence Resource Management Office (manager of the General Defense Intelligence Program); Director, Naval Command, Control, Communications, Computers, Intelligence, Surveillance and Reconnaissance (C4ISR) Scientific and Technical Intelligence (S&TI) analysis at the Office of Naval Intelligence; special assistant to the Associate Director of Central Intelligence for Military Support, and the Chief of Staff for the Director of Military Intelligence Staff. In addition, Terry has directed, conducted, and enabled intelligence operations globally, with much of this work being focused on the requirements, planning, and implementation of intelligence and communications technologies, software, and architectures.

Terry is Chair Emeritus of the Intelligence and National Security Alliance (INSA) Cyber Council, a former member of the AFCEA Intelligence Committee from 2008-2017, former President of Naval Intelligence Professionals (NIP), a 2017/18 Cyber Fellow at New America (nonpartisan think tank), and a member of the USNA Cyber Education Advisory BOD since 2010 and of the Cyber Florida Advisory BOD.

Terry's personal awards include the Office of the Secretary of Defense Medal for Exceptional Civilian Service; the Navy Senior Civilian Award of Distinction; the NGA Personal Medallion for Excellence; the Coast Guard Distinguished Public Service Award; the Director of Central Intelligence National Intelligence Certificate of Distinction; the National Intelligence Reform Medal; and the National Intelligence Meritorious Unit Citation.

PART THREE
Technology

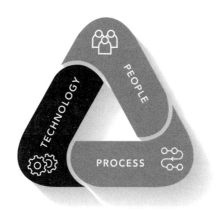

FAST-EVOLVING TECHNOLOGY IN A HYPER-CONNECTED world presents opportunities for growth that we as CISOs must leverage and manage to ensure a successful and secure business. In manufacturing, the once safe-and-siloed operational technology (OT) world is now perimeterless, with sensors and other edges everywhere connected 24/7. These connected devices now expose the OT world to the IT side of the house, raising the risk level exponentially. More third parties, such as supply chain players, are now connected, as are workers via tablets, smartphones, and other devices. Connections are often both on an internal network and in the cloud—in fact, in multiple clouds. All of these changes create more security vulnerabilities across workplace environments than ever before.

When the COVID-19 pandemic hit, our workplaces abruptly moved into our homes. Moving forward, workplaces and personal spaces will merge as work from home becomes the new normal for many. Employees on less secure home networks are attending meetings by video, using collaboration platforms with their teams, and managing company data in the cloud. From a security standpoint, this accelerated blending of work and home, which already had been on our radar as leaders, is even more concerning.

To address all of the issues you face, there are more security solutions available than ever before. But this is a double-edged sword because the proliferation of products and the pace of change in the security solutions market is also challenging for CISOs.

As you know, simply layering the latest security technology onto your enterprise won't get you where you want to go. Can you build in security from the beginning to encompass the entire enterprise? Which emerging security solutions should you consider adopting? What new areas should be considered? What can guide those decisions? A more holistic approach is required.

You need the right technology in place throughout your network. Your security technology must align with a strong architecture to make sure there are no gaps. Your security platform should accommodate point solutions when required but also easily integrate into and across all of your systems.

To keep up with evolving and fast-moving threats, your security technology must be automated. The right technology also must be mature, well supported by the vendor, and capable of helping you achieve the goals of your security processes. To grow with your enterprise, your security must be scalable. Finally, your security must be easy to use out of the box—or your people will find ways to work around or ignore it.

In this section of the book, we cover key areas that merit particular attention from CISOs today, including security in the cloud, IoT and edge security, and security-driven networking. The final chapter in this section offers a look at your most strategic objective: achieving end-to-end security.

Security in the Cloud

While the decision to move to the cloud is straightforward from multiple business angles, working in the cloud requires additional effort and planning with respect to security. Moving to the cloud is further complicated by decisions about which cloud or clouds to adopt: public, private, or hybrid. This requires an understanding of the security characteristics of the cloud in question.

Each cloud has variables, especially regarding security and compliance. How do you handle monitoring in the cloud? You also have to determine who maintains the system: you or a managed service security provider? What are the advantages and disadvantages of each approach? How do you use the shared responsibility model advanced by cloud vendors when, ultimately, the responsibility for security rests squarely with you? Chapter 11 covers the important area of security in the cloud.

IoT and Edge Security

The line between the physical and cyber worlds has disappeared. Whether cyber or physical, whether your data, your point-of-sale systems, or your sensors on the edge, everything is interconnected across your enterprise. Some of this technology, especially IoT and edge technology, was not built with security in mind and may include older network interfaces that are activated without evaluation of the risk of connecting them. You have to look at all your technology—from sensors at the edge to your data center, from your coffee pot to your HVAC system—and make sure you haven't created an open door or even a cracked window into your network.

The connections between the cyber and physical world also help you as a defender. Now that your doors, your locks, and your security cameras are connected in the cyber realm, those connections can help you from a cybersecurity perspective. That cyber and physical integration gives you a better view of what's going on both on your premises and in your network. For example, if you see unusual network activity and correlate that activity with information from your security cameras showing someone entering your data center, you can determine you have more than a cyber problem: you also have either an outside intruder or an insider on premises after hours. We cover security in the converging cyber and physical worlds in Chapter 12.

Security-Driven Networking

Given the critical nature of networks to every aspect of the business, the distinction between security and networking is a false dichotomy. Security policy must be applied across dynamic networks, including SD-WAN. Security-driven networking is based on the idea of bringing security and networking together seamlessly.

Security must be built into the network. You also have to continually adapt to a changing environment. In a world where zero trust is becoming standard security practice, network design must include ways to segment information and processes, specify how to define users, and describe how you handle network access control. From containers to APIs to remote access to 5G, security policies must be applied consistently all across your network, including dynamic edges. Safe remote access, governed by defined security policies, should be available wherever your users are. Security-driven networking is covered in Chapter 13.

Achieving End-to-End Security

The core principles of end-to-end security are speed, agility, interoperability, and continuous monitoring. Achieving end-to-end security requires integrating solutions across your entire network, your physical premises, and in the cloud. As you make effective use of platforms that leverage automation and manage complexity, you must keep the goal of end-to-end security in mind. You also have to address compliance with evolving security regulations, standards, and frameworks.

Finally, when you think you have end-to-end security in place, your work is not done. As you integrate new people, new processes, and new technology, you have to keep security at the forefront. End-to-end security requires building in security from the beginning and ensuring that new technology is integrated in a way that continues to achieve this objective. Chapter 14 covers end-to-end security.

11

Cybersecurity in the Cloud

FATIMA BOOLANI

T HE SHIFT TO THE CLOUD IS UNSTOPPABLE, AND THERE IS NO turning back.

The move away from the "undifferentiated heavy lifting" of running IT stacks and home-grown enterprise software has not only given rise to a tsunami of born-digital startups, but is spurring voracious adoption of cloud computing by companies of all sizes and stripes.

Manifesting in cloud-based front-office application modernization, back-office infrastructure transformation, and software-enabled business process automation, these initiatives are satisfying the intensifying demands for agility, efficiency, and innovation across the modern enterprise. With cloud computing enabling the effective handover of entire technology stacks to third parties—from infrastructure to middleware to applications—companies have been liberated to focus on doing what they do best, which in almost all cases is not procuring, building, administering, and maintaining software and IT plumbing systems.

Yet against this backdrop, the stakes for organizational cyber defense, protection, and response have never been higher. Now, organizations face not only existing threats, but also new cyber obstacles that come with the brave new world of the cloud, characterized by greater vendor and functional fragmentation, as well as increasingly distributed and heterogeneous network architectures.

This comprehensive outsourcing, and straddling of public cloud (Amazon AWS, Microsoft Azure, Google GCP), private cloud (VMware, IBM, Red Hat), hybrid (physical data centers), and cloud productivity applications, has only been accelerated by remote work trends. The result is a metastasizing cyberattack surface, amplifying organizational risk, complexity, and consequently vulnerabilities.

161

Complexity, Meet Vulnerability

Such a decentralized span of control, combined with an increasing desire for IT nimbleness, then creates the cybersecurity catch-22 of the cloud-powered organization: more agility but more cyber blind spots. Furthermore, the novelty of modern cloud apps and infrastructure has also inspired politically, financially, and criminally motivated attackers to weaponize new attack vectors and techniques against this paradigm.

Users want efficiency, instant gratification of IT-as-a-service, and democratized access to all cloud capabilities to enhance business productivity. Meanwhile IT, and not the cloud service providers, are burdened with policing and protecting all the resulting data, configurations, applications, and workloads such demands unleash, while trying to keep organizations safe across an even greater volume and diversity of cyberattack vectors.

Contending with such unfettered choice (APIs, microservices, containers, serverless infrastructure, code repositories, and cloud apps on top), these users often have insufficient knowledge or attention to detail in identifying and prioritizing cybersecurity posture. This is exemplified by rampant user-driven misconfiguration, poor password protocol, loose permission settings, low policy awareness, and a lack of stringent organizational oversight. Consider this in the light of understaffed, overworked, and under-skilled IT personnel employing manual, human-error prone, and legacy approaches ill-suited to surveil and remediate such behavior.

These dynamics at work are plainly apparent in some of the biggest cloud breaches to date—Capital One, Facebook, GoDaddy, Verizon, Docker Hub, WWE, Adobe, Best Western, and select federal agencies. Hundreds of millions of records and petabytes of data were exposed in these cases directly as a result of server and database deployment errors and lax access safeguards, suggesting the principal cause of cloud security and related breach incidents remains user negligence and poor cyber governance.

More (Vendors & Connectivity) But Not Merrier

Yet another facet gating the progress toward a cloud cybersecurity "nirvana" is the steep protect-and-defend learning curve inherent to working with myriad vendors. For example, typical training and implementation documentation guides for just one cloud service could be hundreds of pages long, requiring idiosyncratic configurations to ensure cybersecurity policies are repeatable and harmonious with pre-existing investments and environments.

Layering in the surge of devices and user types on enterprises' IT and operational technology networks only exacerbates this picture. Vulnerable connected devices running unique operating systems and transient users are in tandem increasingly traversing diverse on-premises and cloud architectures. This brings a multitude of unidentified unknowns, challenging IT to secure what is an unabating proliferation of ephemeral resources, assets, and identities.

With this backdrop, the odds necessarily appear stacked against organizations seeking to shield intellectual property from exfiltration by these new, multiplicative attack vectors. A stretched-thin, undertrained, and scarce cybersecurity workforce must yet again contend with suboptimal awareness of evolving cloud security and policies, as well as diminished visibility across all these spheres. The generational expertise gap in cloud versus traditional IT only compounds these issues.

More Risk, Same Budget

Despite the more sophisticated threat landscape and increased risk spawned by cloud uptake, cloud cybersecurity spending remains comparatively low. For perspective, of the more than $60 billion of spending on commercial cybersecurity tools and technologies in 2020, less than 10% was cloud-centric, according to Gartner and public company disclosure. Disregarding the delivery method (security through the cloud, or security SaaS), this proportion shrinks to less than 5% when solely considering solutions dedicated to protecting data and assets in cloud environments (security for the cloud). In the context of public cloud spending swelling to $400 billion in the next several years from $270 billion today, this shallow level of cybersecurity investment is starker still.

Such a disparity is perhaps owed to reticence around the maturity and potency of available solutions, given the embryonic state of the market. Additionally, defense strategies involving familiar on-premises techniques reconditioned for cloud, and funded by refurbished, conventional cybersecurity categories, could also be playing a role. But these revised techniques and solutions are not up to the task of keeping pace with the rapid innovation of cloud service providers' offerings or coping with the staggering data generation and sprawl in these domains. Nor are they proficient in thwarting new and emerging vulnerabilities and threats.

Such new challenges and higher complexity in turn have inspired the creation of the cloud workload protection platforms (CWPP), cloud security posture management (CSPM), and cloud workload segmentation categories. While state-of-the-art, we anticipate these systems augmenting traditional, well-understood vulnerability management, microsegmentation, classic endpoint protection, and systems management functionality. Such unification promises both automated and continuous environmental visibility, iterative or runtime scanning for vulnerabilities and misconfigurations across organizations' diverse IT footprints, and most importantly the steady extension of existing cyber defense skill sets.

Other cloud security challenges include:

- The short-lived nature of cloud resources, making data collection and incident investigation difficult. For example, forensic evidence is lost when resources are terminated or when workloads are decommissioned.

- Multi-cloud usage and portability of cloud resources, decentralizing organizational control across specialized teams and vendors.

- Manual processes ineffective and incompatible with elastic attack surfaces.

- Retrofitted static technologies adding performance drags on workflows and cloud systems in their reliance on reboots, scan storms, and invasive signature updates.

Ultimately, overhauling foundational cybersecurity architecture and design carries inherent operational disruption and technology efficacy risks that few organizations have been bold enough to face. Both cultural (risk aversion, change management hurdles) and experiential limitations (skills deficit in an already tight labor market for cybersecurity professionals) remain the root causes. In the meantime, it is essential that organizations crystallizing adaptive cloud cybersecurity programs in response to new realities, ensuring minor operational lapses from "learning by doing" within highly intricate, multi-faceted IT systems, do not risk disastrous impacts to the broader cybersecurity posture. Sampling the best of the capabilities of emerging specialists, reliable incumbents, and service providers themselves likely portends the most optimal outcome.

Who Is Ultimately Responsible?

As corporate IT systems hasten their migration to third-party cloud providers, the responsibility for cybersecurity often gets lost in the move. Cloud providers have a deliberately limited purview, typically pledging security only for their own underlying infrastructure.

The so-called shared-responsibility cybersecurity paradigms championed by the cloud providers place the onus of protecting critical network, access, application, and data resources on the resident organization. While expeditiously producing à la carte and embedded security services for the core computing, storage, and infrastructure solutions they provide, cloud vendors are largely indemnified for any role played in cloud security incidents and data breaches. Thus, buying organizations relying on these now business-critical capabilities are on the hook to identify and manage the myriad availability, transport, configuration management, and data leakage risks involved on their own.

Moving forward, cloud providers and cloud consuming organizations can more equitably share the risk. Cloud providers ought to elevate their baseline for how much they defend the assets they host, and lead the charge on fostering cross-vendor integration of largely siloed approaches to traffic inspection, data governance, and access compliance. Although this is historically unprecedented, consuming organizations should also demand cybersecurity breach insurance and even warranty-like commitments typical of other service-based industries, particularly as the market power and share of suppliers become concentrated.

Worth highlighting too are organizations such as the Cloud Security Alliance that are defining distinct frameworks, best practices, and standards-based guidelines for ensuring secure cloud computing environments. Since 2009, the not-for-profit Alliance has endeavored to deliver vendor-neutral subject matter research, education, and certifications so that diverse parties can operate in a forum where building and maintaining a trusted cloud ecosystem is the universal goal.

Increased regulatory oversight could also prove beneficial in ensuring greater compliance to higher cybersecurity hygiene standards. HIPAA and PCI-DSS information protection mandates introduced decades ago are salient examples of how such interventions positively influence adherence and build accountability momentum.

By working together, vendors, customers, and consortia such as the Cloud Security Alliance appear best positioned to defend against active cyber adversaries who are exploiting the very technological developments that are advancing the economy.

FATIMA BOOLANI

Fatima Boolani is the co-head of the software equity research team at Citi, with deep experience in the cybersecurity and infrastructure software subsectors. Prior to Citi, Ms. Boolani spent a decade at UBS and Jefferies in a similar capacity, crafting rigorous investment recommendations and thematic industry reports for institutional investors. She began her career on Wall Street as an investment banker in the enterprise software sector at Thomas Weisel Partners. She has earned numerous Honorable Mention accolades in Institutional Investor polls and was named a "Rising Star" in equity research by Business Insider in 2017. She is a graduate of the Ivey School of Business at the University of Western Ontario, where she earned her Honors Business Administration degree with Dean's List distinction.

12

The Convergence of Cyber and Physical
IoT and Edge Security

SONIA E. ARISTA

A S A CISO, YOUR CHALLENGE HAS BEEN FOCUSED ON protecting your enterprise network, devices on that network, the network perimeter, and the work environment—whether that environment is a factory or an office. But for many businesses, the work environment is now merging with the home and leisure space. In 2020, many more workers began working remotely, and some continue to work from home or exotic locations; more than half of all workers surveyed by PwC would now like to work from home at least three days a week.[1] As people continue to rely on edge computing devices in offices and in factories, increasingly work outside the office, use personal devices to perform business tasks, and use cloud-based business apps and software, the traditional network perimeter has been replaced by ubiquitous global edge points.

Strong edge security encompasses visibility, protection, and potentially remediation at the point where data processing is conducted. The same sophisticated operational technology (OT) risks found in environments like manufacturing plants, healthcare facilities, and government infrastructure also can put your enterprise at risk. Protecting data, processes, and people beyond that traditional perimeter—where the cyber and physical converge—is a growing challenge CISOs must address.

Expanding IoT Leads to Expanding Risks

In managing your security program, you may be accustomed to monitoring only the devices, software, and other technology adopted in your enterprise. Internet-connected technology is entering our lives at a fast pace in consumer tech and gaming, healthcare, smart city infrastructure, and industrial IoT. Each internet-enabled device in your workers' environments that has management capability is a new perimeter, or edge, and has the potential for security vulnerabilities. Your workers are using their own devices in the workspace and toggling back and forth between their personal apps/accounts and approved workplace accounts. Device-level vulnerabilities in the home, in a game, or in a nonapproved workplace app can traverse cyber boundaries and put your enterprise at risk. In the interest of being more productive or acclimating to these work-from-home environments, employees are also increasingly using technology that your security team has not adopted or vetted. This trend, coupled with increased digitalization of the work environment overall, is leading to an unmanaged, multiple-edge frontier of cybersecurity risks, resulting in potential breaches or disruption of business.

Connected consumer technology is expanding to many so-called edges in the home, including doorbells, baby monitors, washing machines, dryers, dishwashers, coffee makers, HVAC systems, and more. These household appliances are internet-connected to help manufacturers calibrate remote devices and perform diagnostics and to help consumers optimize energy use. For example, many vehicles are now connected with features including navigation, entertainment, tracking (both for stolen cars and time of use to monitor teenage driving), vehicle-to-vehicle communication, and more. As another example, the gaming industry is increasingly vying for total immersion experiences through wearable technology and other sensory devices.

In hospitals, edge devices monitor patients' vital signs including heart rate, blood pressure, temperature, and glucose level; robots perform surgery; edge devices monitor patient moods; and more. Medical professionals use applications running on edge devices—their own phones and tablets—using Wi-Fi, voice over IP, cellular, and Bluetooth transmission methods to manage and transport data. Each device and transmission method has its own vulnerabilities; moreover since many of those devices are not managed or secured by your network, this creates enormous complexity in the network environment to identify what is trusted or secure.

Sometimes the so-called edge lives in our bodies. Research, development, and use of implanted or ingested medical devices or pharmacology is growing, with tens of millions of people worldwide living with implanted medical devices as of 2001, according to Science Direct. These devices regulate heartbeats; provide diagnostics, for example, glucose levels in the case of diabetic patients; and more. When former Vice President Dick Cheney famously expressed concerns that his pacemaker could be hacked, doctors replacing it were asked to disable the wireless feature. In 2017, the FDA recalled nearly a half-million pacemakers over concerns that the devices could be compromised. These advances are significant in terms of patient treatment and health, but the cybersecurity implications are sobering.

Smart city and utility infrastructure has expanded to include transportation, power supply and transmission, water supply and transmission, and more, all of which open up multiple edge points in the form of smart sensors and other operational technologies. Smart city infrastructure hacks could dovetail with a terrorist attack to combine a physical threat with a disruption of first-responder systems or infrastructure. One well-known attack in 2016 disrupted Ukraine's power grid.[2] Another more recent event occurred in Florida when an unauthorized user had momentary access and attempted to change the formula of the public water supply.[3]

In manufacturing, the newly networked processing and automation functions derived from the rapid digitization of industry have potential vulnerabilities at multiple edge points. Attackers can exploit or manipulate code, override or disrupt data transfer, alter the robots and supporting software, seize control of other machines, and manipulate components at the edge. You probably remember that the Stuxnet attack in 2010[4] temporarily disabled Iran's nuclear program and the 2014 attack on a German steel mill[5] caused major physical damage.

The software involved to communicate with edge points in these sectors, if not properly vetted, updated, and protected, opens up the potential for security risks, especially if data and commands are transmitted over open internet channels. Rapid go-to-market pressures to engineer APIs to promote system integration often reduce the amount of security review performed, and proper due diligence, from a cyber perspective, is overlooked. Bad actors then have the opportunity to manipulate this software through code injection and other techniques to compromise safety, steal personal and financial information, or otherwise cause harm and chaos.

Device-Specific Approach Leads to Increased Risk

As more manufacturers enter the market, they're creating and defining their own edge processing chips and semiconductors, instead of using generic components. For example, Apple released its M1 chip in November 2020, and the company is moving toward consolidating multiple computing functions into one component. The goal is to create a chip optimized with processing specific to the device itself. The data doesn't have to transfer out—to the data center or to the cloud—for computational power or rely on other parties for operating systems to enable the software functionality. Your phone is a perfect example.

Although this strategy supports operational optimization of device functions, this self-contained, device-specific approach creates variability among processing components, which leads to increased complexity, risks, and vulnerabilities. From a security management point of view, this level of variability across all the computational devices in the enterprise will exacerbate two traditional information security challenge areas: patching and supply chain vulnerabilities. Testing and patching in highly proprietary or closed systems relies heavily on manufacturers' release and remediation schedules (think Microsoft). The added variability among components also leads to challenges in visibility and maintenance of these individualized subcomponents and, therefore, more cyber risks in the supply chain.

On the edge, with proximity detonation of exploits, the identification and remediation timeline become nil. As the point of processing moves closer to the edge, these various standards within operating system–specific processors make it harder for cybersecurity professionals to identify indicators of compromise. In many cases, unless an operational disruption or other indicator event occurs, cyber events poised at data theft or data integrity compromise may never be identified by the user or the enterprise.

Moving Toward Solutions: Taking Stock

Another challenge is knowing and understanding all the technology in play in your enterprise. Not only are many companies seeing enormous organic growth of their workforce, but mergers and acquisitions in the last several years have also expanded, as traditional business models are trying to add high-tech enablement to their service portfolio and products.

Companies need to iteratively take stock in terms of knowing what edge devices, software, apps, and code are deployed in their enterprises, including those adopted by employees on their own. Most importantly, these information security programs must be able to scale and accommodate increasing regulatory controls. The current state of international and domestic legislation and industry guidance is woefully behind technological innovation and use.

Finally, a firm understanding of service providers and partners (even those that are used tangentially) to help your operations is critical. For example, after the SolarWinds breach, the question of the day was: are you using SolarWinds? What version, or what modules? Many security leaders did not know and first had to check—not only their environments, but their core service partners. That lack of initial knowledge delays remediation and poses a greater risk.

Defining What You Have

One of the most fundamental gaps in many businesses is that they really haven't taken the time to categorize what constitutes their own intellectual property—many in the industry refer to this as protecting your crown jewels. The rush to beat the competition to market has outweighed management of data integrity controls and assurances. For example, in the software development space, go-to-market pressures mean teams are coding feverishly to release new software and upgrades to meet customer demand. In the process, they take security shortcuts and fail to categorize what they've created, or they keep building on unstable platforms and old infrastructure, accruing enormous technical debt.

Regardless of the type of business or industry vertical, many organizations also have a large pool of unstructured data built up over time, including data acquired from third parties—the unstructured data dilemma.

Although you'd think that a large pool of data would be more likely to yield representational insight, algorithmic bias is a real problem as is the chance that a large subset of data is missing, or perhaps results are skewed and functionality is developed with faulty logic.

Particularly with companies now reselling customer datasets as part of their revenue model, this mining of highly or nonidentified data can pose a big problem and skew results. Getting the right data subset to software architects and engineers—and ensuring those engineers have the right level of access to certain DevOps environments—is critical to ensuring accurate results from AI and ML.

Without the right access and security protocols, data that is iteratively downloaded and uploaded over time could become degraded, contaminated, and vulnerable. This danger has become more intense as large volumes of data dilute the visibility of any, potentially small, contamination. In this environment, data governance is more important than ever.

Further, as noted earlier, your workers are using their own edge devices—phones, tablets, laptops—and often their own apps and software in your enterprise. In the distributed workforce scenario, once an employee initiates or introduces the use of new software or a new device at the edge, the potential for enterprise data leakage, loss, and contamination is significant.

When that new software or device accesses corporate data that is uncategorized, data loss protection tools can't encrypt or otherwise secure that intellectual property—it's available and potentially exposed to bad actors who know where to look. That scenario is the equivalent of putting your personal pictures, your tax documents, or perhaps your coveted research into the equivalent of an open folder on the internet. *You can't protect what you don't know you have.*

Building in the time and processes to categorize data, software, code, processes, and edge devices used in your enterprise will enable your security team to then properly employ data loss protection (DLP) and cloud access security brokers (CASBs) to secure and protect your enterprise's intellectual property.

As a security program implements solutions like CASB and DLP filters within their environment, what they are really trying to gain is improved visibility of enterprise or corporate data. In some cases, there are clear compliance reasons to do this because some subsets of data are protected through federal legislation like HIPAA or industry standards like PCI, and identifying and protecting these data assets is required.

What may be less straightforward is the identification of intellectual property that tends to grow organically over time. Examples include research data, source code, client databases, and data in edge devices. This proliferation of metadata growing exponentially poses challenges regarding management, retention, access, and distribution. But in the last several years, increased activity across all market segments related to mergers creates even greater challenges such as designation of ownership or—more pointedly—security. It is incredibly difficult for organizations to keep account of all the data they are chartered to protect.

Baselining Normal Function and Behavior

For a long time, the security industry has been moving away from signature-based type detection and remediation tactics to more applied analytics and behavioral analysis as it relates to the edge. Technologies gaining traction, and that are able to be applied at scale, focus on baselining what an object's normal state of function is and using applied analytics to determine how a person, device, or operating system normally acts. Then, those technologies look for aberrations or out-of-bounds behavior as indicators of compromise from a cybercrime perspective. The ideal security technologies are able to examine nuances of behavior and context to find even minor aberrations, alert the enterprise to that activity, and optimally apply a quarantine or other remediation tactic automatically.

AI and ML Can Track Security Trends on the Edge

Sophisticated threat actors and cyber criminals are actively using AI and machine learning. The good news: these same technologies also offer new advantages for defenders. Information on emerging and troubling security trends and insight derived from machine learning and AI can be leveraged by being directly synced to modern IT infrastructure. Many organizations are focused on industry-specific trending—identifying threats that have a high probability of exploit, in certain markets. Leveraging machine-learned insight to drive toward auto-remediation is fundamental in ensuring low-level threats are thwarted, and teams can focus on remediation for more complex (and business detrimental) incidents. Invest in AI- and ML-driven information services that will provide your enterprise, and its edge points, with this valuable aggregation of widely focused and industry-specific security intelligence.

Identifying Acceptable and Unacceptable Risks

Just as it is recommended to categorize data and devices, individual enterprises must define how they categorize risk. As a security leader, you have to determine what vulnerabilities you can potentially live with and what risks are never acceptable.

Mature information security programs are hypersensitized to what constitutes smart risk (that which the business chooses to accept in the interim or long term to achieve a strategy or outcome) versus risks that can be opportunistically exploited and are simply grounded in poor process, policy, or governance. The latter should be defined as unacceptable risk and have the required governance structure to support reduction of these risks or, even better, elimination.

CISOs must look beyond defined technical risk; it is imperative to categorize the risk in the context of the business or operational implications. For example, as a hospital CISO you may be able to accept the risk of your servers not being 100% covered by antivirus protection 24/7 but you know you can't tolerate any risk associated with an edge device that's about to go into the operating room and be implanted in a patient. In this context, investment, prioritization and the depth of a security risk assessment is clear.

Determining Responsibility and Liability for Security

Securing edge devices' data, software, and code up and down your supply chain is a critical issue. As evidenced in recent high-profile incidents, a vulnerability in one link of a supply chain can be detrimental to the entire supply chain. As a CISO, ensure that your program incorporates proper due diligence of partners to determine their security practices including programs and policies, as well as technology investments in understanding their edge points, data sets, data flows and network flows. These practices will impact the integrity and security of the data output sold or provided to your enterprise.

Carefully read your agreements with SaaS providers to make sure you know who is responsible and liable for a security breach, and delineate where the guardianship of data lies at each point in the data exchange. You may not be protected for breaches in your cloud apps and software. Many SaaS providers, even those with security controls, have stringent positions within their contracts that specify that the security controls and the parameters lie within the responsibility of the tenant, which is your enterprise, and not the provider itself.

Conclusion

When it comes to information security, it is widely accepted that market technological advancement and digitalization of business is happening at a rate far outpacing tools and strategies for effective management. Security leaders recognize that they are not able to rely on legislation, certification, and regulatory standards to adequately protect their enterprise environments from cyber threats that may severely impact the business. For the last several years, the discussion has been on the manner in which cloud computing changed the paradigm of processing and storage, but the next decade of computing will be focused on device-level and network-edge processing and, in turn, strategies of effective protection.

Data protection strategies must accommodate visibility of the full data life cycle and constantly evolve and leverage advanced AI- and ML-based tech to achieve remediation at cyber-relevant speeds. As discussed, the advancement of edge-based processing and devices with increased computational power is achieving tremendous operational efficiencies in business, municipal infrastructure, and even our own domestic lifestyles—but threat detection and data security programs must evolve accordingly.

Notes

1. https://www.pwc.com/us/en/library/covid-19/us-remote-work-survey.html

2. https://wired.com/2016/03/inside-cunning-unprecedented-hack-ukraines-power-grid/

3. https://www.wired.com/story/oldsmar-florida-water-utility-hack/

4. https://www.wired.com/2014/11/countdown-to-zero-day-stuxnet/

5. https://www.wired.com/2015/01/german-steel-mill-hack-destruction/

SONIA E. ARISTA

Sonia Arista serves as Vice President and Chief Information Security Officer (CISO) at Everbridge, with global oversight of operational and product security and compliance. She brings over twenty years in IT program management and consulting in the areas of governance, risk, and compliance, with the last fifteen years focused on enterprise data protection.

Prior to joining Everbridge, Sonia was the Healthcare CISO and vertical lead for Fortinet and was the CISO at Tufts Medical Center and the Floating Hospital for Children where she was responsible for the development and management of information security programs. She has also been contracted to serve as an interim CISO for several healthcare-related entities like Wellforce, Nuance Communications, and Verscend Technologies. Her experience in information security leadership includes board-level advisement, incident response, and rapid program alignment to support growth associated with mergers and acquisitions.

Originally from Houston, Sonia graduated from Southern Methodist University in Dallas with a Bachelor of Arts and a Bachelor of Business Administration, then moved to the Boston area twenty years ago. She recently completed her Executive Masters in Cybersecurity at Brown University. She volunteers her time as a mentor to young professionals seeking a career in security and guest lectures for organizations promoting women in STEM and minority advancement.

13 | Security-Driven Networking

LAURA DEANER

T HE DIGITAL WORLD HAS CHANGED AROUND US AS HAVE THE threats. But many organizations continue to operate with a mindset of legacy protection, believing themselves protected by perimeter firewalls. If we define the network only as a way to create the fastest routes, we give attackers a huge advantage. Security-driven networking is the broad idea that for cybersecurity to work properly, the network must be smarter and provide more inherent security.

Ultimately, security should be built deeply into a smarter, faster network. But that won't happen in the near term. In the meantime, cybersecurity professionals must take responsibility for advancing the implementation of security-driven networking. To move forward, we must determine how the network should be smarter and how that intelligence should be distributed across different parts of a more secure network.

In this chapter, we explain how the cloud has changed secure networking, discuss why last-generation solutions won't work, and outline the necessary steps CISOs must take to meet today's cybersecurity challenges and to build true security-driven networking.

The Cloud Has Changed Everything About Security

Over the last twenty years, organizations have moved from experimenting with one cloud to adopting multi-cloud to moving a majority of workloads to the cloud. In the meantime, people in a variety of professions are increasingly working remotely. Even when people are physically in the workplace, they are conducting business on personal devices along with or instead of company equipment.

This evolving work environment has given birth to multiple unknown unknowns. CISOs don't immediately know what operating system or antivirus protection people are using on personal devices and whether that protection is up to date. CISOs don't immediately know whether employees are working on public Wi-Fi in a coffee shop. CISOs don't immediately know whether employees are misusing data or even accessing information they're not entitled to see.

With threats becoming more and more advanced, CISOs must work with all technology teams to build security into the target state and know immediately who and what—including APIs, service accounts, and bots— is accessing the data they are responsible for protecting. Often when an outside server is talking to an enterprise server, that outside server may have privileged access by default to access the enterprise server. Opportunistic threat actors can discover that privileged service account, access the account, and do major damage on the server.

Outside the organization, the threat landscape has become more pervasive with highly motivated, serious threat actors. Malicious nation-states, sophisticated criminal organizations, and other opportunists are launching destructive attacks and using ransomware, targeted phishing campaigns, and a growing number of other techniques.

The proliferation in the number of different cloud services has also complicated security in many ways. We don't have just one cloud. We have cloud for IaaS (infrastructure as a service) like Amazon Web Services, Google Cloud Platform, and Microsoft Azure; cloud for PaaS (platform as a service) like the various programming services on those three clouds; cloud for SaaS (software as a service) such as Salesforce and thousands of other SaaS applications; and then the data center, which in effect has become just another destination that a user may want to or must get to and that can be protected with the same paradigm as these other cloud data centers.

In each of these situations, the challenge is not merely connecting to these different types of clouds, but also making sure that these clouds are used properly. For example, allowing everybody to securely connect to OneDrive or Google Drive is one issue, but preventing data leakage caused by inappropriately sharing files from those drives is an additional security concern. This is just one example of the kind of cloud security capability that is new, is not handled by legacy technology, and must be supported by built-in mechanisms.

Last-Generation Security Solutions Are Inadequate

In this fast-evolving cyber world where many people and organizations are moving to the cloud, a perimeter-based, moat-and-castle approach to security no longer protects your organization. Network security, endpoint security, and application security—all functioning independently without communicating— are failing to protect enterprises that rely on these solutions.

The work environment, the tools used in that environment, and the shifting locations of that environment are all changing quickly. The perimeter that was once the foundation of cybersecurity? Gone. The work-from-home (WFH) surge has brought old problems to light and created new challenges.

Imagine a user is sitting in a Starbucks trying to access their work services. They use single sign-on (SSO) for Microsoft 365, but SaaS applications such as Salesforce or Workday not integrated with the same SSO will require a separate set of credentials—leading us to question whether we should really call this single sign-on to begin with. Further complicating matters, users may access their personal accounts such as Gmail or Dropbox. If users urgently need to send a work document but can't manage to sign in properly, they are likely to circumvent security and use those services instead as a way to get their work done. It's easy to see how this leads to data leakage.

The WFH trend is just one way the security landscape has become acutely complex. With a legacy approach, either not enough security is available or the security is available but poses too much difficulty. Here's how that has become problematic:

- Some organizations seek to boost security via hairpinning. Traffic is routed from the user's location back in through a private network to the data center and then back to the internet, preserving protections. But hairpinning causes performance problems, complicates the network architecture, and doesn't solve issues such as securing access from remote locations.

- Within the perimeter, some organizations are still granting unlimited access to users. Once these users gain access under the legacy paradigm, they get access not only to a specific application for a specific purpose but also to the whole range of the network protected by the firewall. This practice enables large security vulnerabilities.

- VPNs can provide additional security to remote workers as part of hairpinning solutions. But VPNs require the user to do a lot more of the connecting to the network, and a single user might need more than one VPN. Also, as we discuss next, the service-level agreements for VPNs are not designed to handle the large amount of traffic generated by the increase in remote workers.

During the pandemic-fueled surge in remote work, most networks found they couldn't handle the increased load. VPNs crashed multiple times. People couldn't do their jobs because they couldn't get onto the network, so workers, and sometimes security leaders, came up with workarounds that likely weren't secure.

For example, to reduce the load on the remote working infrastructure, some organizations found themselves granting exceptions to security policies, sometimes for a specific (and relatively long) amount of time such as 100 days. Patch management had to be modified to very specific low-load timeframes. Internet gateway technology had to be swiftly updated for local routes to reduce traffic.

Collaboration software, which was once used mostly within the firewall perimeter, had to be updated to enable usage, temporarily, without a VPN but with security policies enabled. Password syncing also came front and center because end users could not enter a physical office to log in to their legacy environments.

End-user computer support teams had to think and react quickly to the scale of laptops being physically sent out and passwords synced and updated en masse. New technologies had to be added to the legacy technologies to properly protect the "keys to the kingdom."

The home environment also had to be updated as an extension of the office. For those working on sensitive topics, smart speakers were moved out of the home office as a precaution. Home routers became managed by end-user computing groups who in an office environment would be responsible only for company-owned technology. This required a huge dissemination of knowledge about information security practices to all frontline teams.

How Security Products Should Adapt

In the meantime, your people are clamoring for more technology and more applications so they can be more effective in their roles. But many vendors are not embedding security into their products—leaving it up to clients to figure out security on their own. For example, how do you integrate Box or Microsoft 365 into a software-defined wide area network (SD-WAN)? In many cases, the desire for speed and convenience is allowed to supersede security.

To protect their environments using legacy tools, CISOs would have to apply controls at every layer that comes to mind: the physical layer, the data link layer, the transport layer, the session layer, and the network layer. That approach takes a lot of time, is not agile, does not allow people to move freely among cloud environments, does not allow people to use a temporary virtual environment, and stifles innovation. If you overlook or skip even one layer or step, threat actors can find a way to infiltrate and get to the data they are after.

One clear solution is the principle of least access, applied to human users as well as to service accounts and APIs. Dole out privileged accounts sparingly and give users, service accounts, and APIs access only to what they need to do their jobs or to perform the needed service.

Similarly, when you allow users inside your network perimeter, allow those users access only to your VLAN and no more.

In addition, the current network architecture is not serving us well:

- Instead of people connecting through a private network that routes traffic to and from the internet, a better architecture is one with points of presence distributed around the world. With that architecture, people, wherever they are, can connect to those points of presence, identify themselves, and then receive—with technology that's as close as possible to those points of presence—the security services they need. The entire network architecture must change to a distributed form.

- Instead of a perimeter-based system where data is easily visible and unprotected inside the castle, today's security model encrypts that data and protects it within individual, often application-based repositories. Instead of a castle and moat, envision armed knights within locked rooms inside that castle.

- Instead of connecting to a network or zone, workers connect to a specific application for a specific purpose—a segment of a network or zone. The necessary network is created at the time of connection. That network understands who each individual is, what they want to do, what they have access rights and permission to do, and then creates one path to get there.

In fact, you might have multiple paths created every session. For example, if a user connects to a point of presence that also has attached security services, there might be one connection that goes over the public internet if the user is accessing their personal Gmail account, and that connection might have very little security associated with it. Another connection might be to a mission-critical application and thus would be routed over a network that has a much higher SLA (service-level agreement), much stronger encryption, and a variety of security services such as data loss prevention and user behavior analytics associated with it. Another connection might be to a third-party SaaS application in which the use of the application is being monitored by a CASB (cloud access security broker) so the user's behavior is tracked. SD-WAN technologies are also important.

Future-Proofing: How CISOs Should Adapt

You don't know what the next crisis will be, but new disasters are on the horizon. The biggest lessons for CISOs from the pandemic include:

- Test and test again. Spend time testing your critical infrastructure on threats, disaster recovery, and business continuity in various scenarios, including scenarios that at first may seem unlikely.

- Know your unknowns. Seek out things you don't know about your environment, the unknown unknowns. Find them before they foul you up.

- Identify your critical assets, including hardware, software, data, and especially critical personnel. Develop plans to mitigate and manage problems with hardware, software, and data. Make contingency and succession plans for essential personnel.

- Think strategy and security. Think about your work strategy as a company and how security will integrate into that strategy, including remote work locations, software for teams, communication, and collaboration in the next crisis, whatever that crisis may be.

- Hire or consult with experts as needed to improve security, safeguard employees' health, and more. Keep in mind that mental health matters.

Protecting Data: What, Where, Who, and How

Eliminating unknown unknowns is critical. To successfully defend your data and your organization against these threats, CISOs must adopt today's mindset of zero trust and assume that threats, from both employees and outsiders, are already inside the network.

Protecting data is paramount. But first, CISOs must know what data they have and which data needs to be protected.

But not all data needs equal protection. CISOs also must adopt today's tools and techniques to tag and protect data.

Take the following steps to protect your data—no matter where it lives—and establish security-aware data routing:

- Begin by identifying and tagging your data based on the level of security required: public, nonpublic, proprietary/IP, or confidential/governed by privacy regulations. Pay particular attention to the most valuable targets in your asset inventory.

- Identify where the data lives: cloud, multi-cloud, and/or on-premises servers.

- Establish and limit who has access to each level of data; for example, only the HR team needs to know employees' private data.

- Set boundaries on behavior; for example, by limiting employees' access to nonpublic organization data if they are on public Wi-Fi or by defining acceptable role-based behavior. Limit behavior/data access that is not within norms.

Now that you've identified, tagged, and established proper routing for your data, encrypt it end-to-end. Congratulations: at that point, your data is no longer an unknown unknown.

Steps to Security-Driven Networking

As you begin the transition to security-driven networking, build support from corporately funded decision-makers by generating metrics that show security events and their root causes, as well as security events that were avoided and why.

Here are steps to take, depending on the security level you want to attain:

Basic:

- Take stock of what you have.
- Even though a perimeter-based system is not effective, you still must define and understand your perimeter.
- Define where your organization's data lives and where its data goes.
- Classify and tag your data based on how securely the information needs to be protected.
- Identify all of your cloud environments, what data resides in each, who can access each cloud, and for what purpose.
- Implement specific strategies to fight phishing and malware.
- Establish a core inspection point for all data.
- Establish a budget for cyber investment.

Better:

- Add more context and layers to that core inspection point.
- Bring in more monitoring.
- Adopt the principle of least access.
- Add intelligent technologies that integrate security event management.
- Establish breach protection.
- Begin monitoring privileged accounts and add technology that alerts when users access data they don't need or behave in ways that are outside norms.
- Determine your cyber risk appetite and establish oversight of third-party risk.
- Evaluate your overall IT spend, including upgrading of disparate and legacy systems and processes.

Best:

- Build zero trust by putting identities in certain categories.

- Disable legacy VPN technologies and then consolidate/standardize VPN technology based on what works in a digital environment.

- Enable more SD-WAN technologies.

- Replace egress firewalls with unified firewalls.

- Add single sign-on, proxies, and data loss prevention.

- Create an incident response playbook.

- Begin regular desktop security exercises and penetration testing.

- Add cyber insurance.

- Benchmark your organization's relative cyber maturity against your peers.

- Create an environment where the CISO can see everything going on via a single pane of glass in a dashboard.

What Does the Best Security-Driven Network Look Like?

The best security-driven network is not one-size-fits-all nor is it a package you can buy and deploy from a vendor. Your security-driven network will be unique to your environment, offering a risk-based approach that's a step forward from your current state. In this environment, you will have removed risk and factored out known unknowns, either by making them knowns or by making them irrelevant.

Once you've created a security-driven network, your job isn't over. This isn't a set-it-and-forget-it exercise. As you add new applications, products, processes, and people, you have to ensure that you and your people continue to integrate security controls.

You may have created an environment where your workers can safely use the public internet. Whether they can work at Starbucks is up to you.

LAURA DEANER

As CISO, Laura Deaner is accountable for establishing and steering Northwestern Mutual's enterprise-wide information risk management and security strategy. In this role she champions an integrated risk culture, driving effective operation of technical and administrative controls. Laura works closely with the executive leadership and the Board of Trustees, matching effective controls to an appropriate level of risk tolerance.

Prior to coming to Northwestern Mutual early in 2021, Laura was CISO at S&P Global, responsible for establishing and driving the enterprise information security vision and program. She leverages her twenty-one years working in security at multinational Fortune 500 companies to build effective information security programs that align deep technical expertise with executive business vision. She was previously the first named CISO at PRNewswire, where she built a comprehensive security practice from the ground up.

Laura holds a BS in computer science from Old Dominion University. She is a member of several cybersecurity and technology societies including OWASP, WiCyS, (ISC)², and Society of Women Engineers (SWE). She's featured in *Women Know Cyber: 100 Fascinating Females Fighting Cybercrime.*

Laura is an advocate for diversity and inclusion in technology as well as her field of cybersecurity. She served as a council member of the S&P Global Diversity Equity and Inclusion Council. Her accomplishments as a council member have included revamping the Employee Resource Groups by adding sentiment- and data-driven metrics to enhance the community goals. She worked to establish partnerships to build in diverse talent pipelines in the technology organizations such as Girls Who Code.

Laura is a frequently requested speaker and respected thought leader, recognized for her innovative leadership and strong business acumen. She has participated in the World Economic Forum's Global Futures Council on Cyber Security as a co-chair leading a group of subject matter experts in solving cyber challenges. She serves on the Board for the Financial Services Information Sharing and Analysis Center (FS-ISAC).

Laura loves spending time with her family. She and her partner Murray are proud parents of four boys. They live in Brooklyn, New York, where they love getting outdoors as a family for hiking, bike rides, and amateur astronomy star gazing. She is also a big fan of science fiction and tinkering with technology at home. Don't ask her how many Raspberry Pis she has.

14

Achieving
End-to-End Security

RENEE TARUN

D
IGITAL INNOVATION BRINGS MORE OPPORTUNITIES—AND
increased risk. As the security perimeter expands, billions of security
edges are formed; numerous devices that were not accessible in
the past are now connected, opening the door to a new wave of
sophisticated threats. The complexity of the ecosystem used by even moderately
sized companies has become incredibly hard to manage, exacerbated further
by the cybersecurity skills gap that has been with us for many years. Sixty-five
percent of organizations already said they lacked sufficient resources, even
before the 2020 pandemic. On top of this, data and processes are subject to
standards and compliance regulations from global, national, regional, local,
and industry entities.

Achieving end-to-end security is more challenging than ever because
today's perimeter is no longer easily defined. With the explosion of remote
working, cloud adoption, and more connected devices than ever, the network
perimeter has expanded beyond the traditional data center. The result of all of
this is billions of edges that need to be secured. (We covered edge security in
Chapter 12.)

At the same time, inspecting network traffic for malicious content has
become nearly impossible. According to Google, more than 80% of traffic is
now encrypted in transit. The adversaries that generate that malicious traffic
are constantly looking for opportunities to exploit any potential weakness in our
infrastructures. At the same time, the attacks are becoming more sophisticated
and costly. Today's organizations are challenged by not only having to deal
with reasonably well understood advanced threats, but also with increasingly
sophisticated unknown threats.

Cyber-threat actors take advantage of the broader digital threat surface and launch innovative new threats as well as tried-and-true attacks. Breaches and ransomware incidents continue to increase. The average cost of a data breach was $3.9 million in 2019, according to the Ponemon Institute, and there's no indication that attacks are slowing down—quite the opposite.

The bad actors use AI to develop exploits and create brand new zero-day attacks faster than ever before. Cybercriminal organizations have invested in building scalable platforms that enable them to launch threatening campaigns by allowing them to pick the malware, the exploits, the botnets, and spam options, and then automate the delivery of those attacks.

Yesterday's Solutions Don't Solve Today's Problems

Many enterprises have responded to growing security threats by adding more of what worked well in the past: security solutions that target single problems. Last-generation solutions no longer work in today's environment. These point solutions have become the Achilles' heel of a complex cybersecurity landscape. The average enterprise deploys 47 different security solutions, according to the Ponemon Institute. Many of these solutions work independently, creating multiple silos to operate and maintain. Siloed systems make it difficult to correlate events and develop a coordinated response. Such systems also create potential security gaps. Multiple point solutions are costly and challenging to manage and maintain.

Each of these solutions generates alerts that are a nightmare to monitor and prioritize, let alone coordinate. The resulting enterprise ecosystems become increasingly complicated with too many vendors, too many alerts, and not enough skilled people to respond to cyber threats in real time. Finding professionals who can operate and maintain a myriad of tools is also a challenge; when these skilled people leave the organization, it creates gaps.

To assemble a set of solutions, many enterprises moved from point solutions to suites of products that offered more capabilities than single point solutions did. Suites are a step toward integration in theory, but in practice, they often include one really good solution while the rest are simply mediocre. As a result, such suites don't offer true end-to-end security. Instead of solving security problems, these suites and point solutions require more human monitoring, pose a challenge to adopting new technologies, and create numerous potential points of failure. They also add cost, maintenance, and operational burdens for security and networking teams who are already understaffed and overworked. Overall, the lack of integration can cause delays in implementation, slower returns on investment, and a higher total cost of ownership.

Since criminal enterprises are using scalable platforms for their attacks, organizations must fight fire with fire. As enterprises strive for speed and scale, cybersecurity leaders will seek to move beyond cybersecurity point solutions and suites and invest in carefully crafted, fully integrated security platforms. This is the real meaning of end-to-end security, a strategy and implementation approach that stands a chance of getting ahead of the challenges just mentioned.

While each organization needs to define a comprehensive and adaptable security posture to meet their needs, there are some fundamental capabilities required for end-to-end security that every organization should consider.

End-to-end security encompasses three driving forces:

- A broad view of the entire threat vector

- Automation

- A full integration of cybersecurity solutions across the network

The rest of this chapter explores key capabilities, including key features to look for as you evolve your platform.

Unified Threat Intelligence

Unified threat intelligence is critical to face today's threats because, to succeed, threat intelligence must reach outside of your organization to your entire industry sector and beyond. You need to know the nature of threats you face before the attackers target your enterprise. Threat intelligence must be timely, accurate, and actionable. Achieving end-to-end security requires incorporating threat intelligence in every component, unified and integrated across the platform.

With an advanced solution that incorporates global data about emerging threats, new mitigation strategies, and best practices, you stand a better chance of remaining ahead of threat adversaries. Unified threat intelligence is foundational and must inform all of the end-to-end security capabilities described in this chapter.

Integrated Security Platforms Enable and Protect Digital Innovation

One key theme throughout this chapter is the need for integration. Making use of unified threat intelligence and any of the other critical capabilities described can work only if each component is relying on a security fabric. End-to-end security would be impossible if every component had to provide its own threat intelligence or integrate with another system. Rather, key capabilities like threat intelligence must be integrated, not bolted on afterward.

Fully integrated security platforms offer critical capabilities in one package, including speed in detecting intrusions, lower cost of ownership, and a higher return on investment—allowing companies to save on staffing and maintenance.

Open platforms are designed as fully integrated but can also incorporate existing solutions so that enterprises don't have to rip and replace.

Building blocks for end-to-end security platforms include technology solutions for security-driven networking, zero-trust access, dynamic cloud protection, and AI-driven security operations. These functions are informed by threat intelligence, driven by AI/automation, and managed through a single pane of glass.

Security-Driven Networking

Traditional network architecture and design tended to build out network access first and then layer on security—essentially treating them as two separate domains. Today's dynamic work environments require a network that enables any person using any device to access any resource from any location. In addition, highly competitive markets inspire organizations to deliver optimized user experiences for their customers and employees while still providing adequate security.

As we discussed in more depth in Chapter 13, security-driven networking converges networking and security. When security is woven into the network core, networks can evolve and expand to meet the digital demand while reducing risk. This approach enables a highly flexible and adaptable environment that can support innovation and leverage technology trends such as hyperscale computing, multi-cloud environments, and 5G.

Traditional (WAN) architectures are often plagued with issues such as latency and slow performance when accessing cloud services. In addition, organizations continue to pay high MPLS costs for WAN transport that delivers a suboptimal user experience.

Software-defined WAN (SD-WAN) solutions are increasingly popular for organizations. Such solutions simplify the management and operation of a WAN, reduce costs, and enable direct cloud access at remote branches, thus eliminating backhauling traffic (routing all branch office traffic through the data center). SD-WAN improves performance by prioritizing business-critical traffic and real-time services.

Most SD-WAN solutions provide basic firewall and virtual private network (VPN) functions. However, they are often not sufficient, thus forcing IT teams to layer on additional security that increases complexity, creates more points of failure, and increases costs. Instead, organizations should look for secure SD-WAN solutions that provide a wide range of integrated security features, such as next-generation firewall, intrusion prevention, encryption, antivirus, and sandboxing capabilities. When you take an approach that combines these functions, you gain better performance, accelerated network and security convergence, consistent network and security policies, and operational efficiencies.

In the past, organizations required workers located outside of the office to connect directly back to the core network to access cloud applications and data. Enterprises today are struggling to adopt converged security and networking strategies to address dominant trends including:

- The prevalence of multi-cloud environments.

- A more remote, distributed workforce working from cloud applications and accessing internal data, which can result in inconsistent security and network policies and enforcement mechanisms.

- The need for user experience improvements and workflow optimization, as 70% of users prefer working remotely but still report network performance issues.

These trends are driving the need for secure access services edge (SASE)—a security and networking solutions bundle delivered at the cloud edge via a cloud-native architecture. As defined by Gartner, SASE converges networking and security technologies and enables flexible consumption for users wherever they are—both on and off the network.

SASE solutions can provide:

- Consistent protection at the network edge
- Application of firewall and security policies regardless of user location
- The ability to shift from a CapEx to an OpEx model to lower costs and decrease complexity

Zero-Trust Access

Many organizations struggle with security today because they don't necessarily know exactly who and what is on their networks in the first place; they don't have visibility and control. If you can't see it, you can't protect it. In today's world, employees and customers need access anytime, anywhere, from any device. No matter where they're working, when they're working, or what they're working with, your workforce needs continuous monitoring and protection.

Traditionally, enterprises have worried more about cyberattacks from outside the network than about malicious or accidental threats posed by insiders. But an increasing number of attacks and compromises involve people and devices already inside the network.

There is no longer a network perimeter, no inside or outside. Monitoring must extend to two areas that previously weren't high-profile concerns: the inside of the network (once presumed safe) and a proliferation of endpoints at the edge (which didn't exist before).

Organizations are now faced with more IoT and OT devices connecting into the network, such as card readers, vending machines, and ventilation systems. These "headless" devices were not built with security in mind and are often connected without the knowledge of security and IT, making the organization vulnerable to more threats.

Leaders must shift their mindset to view every user and device as inherently untrustworthy, regardless of where they are. Requests by users and devices for access to resources are granted only after the user or device has been verified. This approach is referred to as a zero-trust model (ZTA).

Implementing a zero-trust access approach focuses on having visibility and control over who and what is connecting to the network. It requires implementing controls to identify, authenticate, and monitor users and devices whether they are on or off the network. You must continuously verify all users as they access corporate applications and data. You must also be able to identify, classify, and profile every device on your network. Similarly, people and devices should have access only to what is absolutely needed, following the principle of least privilege. That involves segmentation, separation of duties, and need to know only access.

When it comes to implementing ZTA for users, organizations must verify every user attempting to gain access and what role they play within the organization—are they an employee, a contractor, a guest, a partner, and so on. Single sign-on authentication helps to prevent password fatigue for users.

Since usernames and passwords are often a prime target for adversaries and are often compromised, organizations need to consider an additional layer of authentication such as multi-factor authentication. Once a user is authenticated, role-based access control (RBAC) gives users access rights and services based upon their specific role within the organization.

Organizations have more devices than ever connecting to their environments, including an influx of business-enabled IoT devices and organizations adopting bring your own device (BYOD) policies. Security teams need to have visibility into all these devices to see their type, function, and purpose for being on the network. Network access control (NAC) technologies can help implement ZTA by enabling security teams to discover and classify devices, establish proper access controls, and provide continuous monitoring and remediation to threats before they spread to the rest of the network.

The zero-trust model also works for applications. Zero-trust network access (ZTNA) creates brokered access to applications for users. It's a way of controlling access to applications regardless of where the user or the application resides. Applications can be in data centers or in the cloud, and users can be in the office or working remotely.

Traditional remote access was handled by VPNs that provide unrestricted access to the network, based on the premise that once a user or device passes network perimeter controls, they are presumed to be trusted. On the contrary, ZTNA takes the approach that no user or device can access anything until they prove themselves trustworthy. Therefore, organizations should evolve their remote access from VPNs to a ZTNA solution. Such solutions can provide a better user experience and provide a more granular set of security protections.

Today's increasing threats require zero-trust access to be more than a buzzword; it must be an integral part of your security architecture. Since locking down the network is rarely a viable option, you have to balance security and accessibility to be successful. Zero-trust access makes it simpler for CISOs to discover all the users and devices accessing the network and to manage their associated security risks.

AI-Driven Security Operations

Humans, even the best security analysts, don't have the time or ability to sift through and comprehend the massive landscape of data and to perform manual detection correlation. The vast amount of unaggregated security data makes it hard to see what's happening and prioritize threats.

The average SOC receives more than 10,000 alerts per day, and the large enterprises see more than 150,000 alerts per day. Meanwhile, IT teams are understaffed or undertrained (due to the cybersecurity skills gap) and can't keep up with the alerts. Yet these teams ignore or overlook alerts at their peril: a single alert may be the difference between detecting and thwarting a major incident and missing it entirely. In addition, the need to demonstrate compliance with security and privacy standards and laws takes precious time away from threat identification and response.

A platform powered by AI and machine learning can help discern and respond to threats in real time. AI and automated tools simplify network management across these environments, alert security teams to imminent threats, and process an automatic threat response. AI can continuously sift through mountains of data collected from devices to identify threats. It can also automatically investigate the influx of alerts that traditionally required manual input from security teams, enabling teams to be more efficient. AI-powered platforms free security teams to spend more time honing strategy, researching advanced threats, and cultivating a cyber-aware culture.

As security teams face a continuously expanding threat landscape and more complex environments, throwing more bodies at the problem does not scale. Therefore, organizations need to adopt key AI-driven and automated capabilities to facilitate fast and effective security operations. This array of technologies includes endpoint security, advanced threat protection such as sandboxing and security operations platforms such as SOAR, endpoint protection, and extended detection and response (XDR).

Endpoint Security Solutions

An endpoint is the last line of defense in many ways. It's your laptop, your phone, and your smart device that downloads updates. At enterprise scale, endpoints include all such devices, both corporate issued and personal devices used for work.

Endpoint detection and response (EDR) solutions can identify threats in your network and then respond to those threats. An EDR solution can analyze the nature of the threat and give your IT team information about how the threat was initiated, which parts of your network it attacked, the current status, and how to stop the attack.

EDR solutions target advanced threats that, because they are engineered to get past primary defenses, get into your environment. EDR solutions further protect your network by containing the threat and preventing it from spreading.

Of course, it is better to stop threats before they get that far. An endpoint protection platform (EPP) targets threats as they enter your network to shut them down before they compromise any endpoint on your network. However, it is nearly impossible for an EPP to provide 100% protection and keep all threats from penetrating your systems. You must be able to do remediation. Therefore, an effective endpoint security strategy often includes both EDR and EPP.

Sandboxing

Sandboxing protects your network and your enterprise by setting up a test area or "sandbox" to see if particular code is deemed safe or unsafe. It confines malware and malicious code to an area separate from the rest of your network. A malware sandbox restricts the actions of an application to this isolated environment. Within this safe zone, the sandbox analyzes the behavior of an object. If something bad happens, it affects only the sandbox and not the other computers and devices on the network. In parallel, any malicious code is quarantined in the sandbox so it does not spread to the rest of the enterprise.

Security Orchestration, Automation, and Response (SOAR)

At a basic level, security operations focuses on looking at various logging, reporting, and analytics, often from multiple panes of glass. As organizations mature, they require a security architecture that enables the unified collection and analysis of data from diverse information sources and multivendor tools, including logs, performance metrics, security alerts, and configuration changes.

For most organizations, this requires security information and event management (SIEM) capabilities to collect and analyze data combined with a distributed event correlation engine to enable complex event pattern detection. The next phase is automated responses through SOAR technologies, which allow separate security components to communicate and interoperate.

SOAR solutions combine three software capabilities: managing threats and vulnerabilities, responding to security incidents, and automating security operations. SOAR solutions in a security platform allow organizations to collect data about security threats, correlate information, and then automatically respond to security events in real time without human intervention. SOAR solutions identify threats and implement a response strategy. The system is automated, to the extent possible, to make it run more efficiently. SOAR solutions empower your team by enriching data with context.

SOAR solutions offer faster incident response and standardize and scale processes that improve security and reduce business risks and costs. An effective SOAR solution remediates the flooding of alerts, reduces repetitive manual processes, and augments tasks by filling in the gap where resources are limited. Teams can create automated playbooks versus having to write scripts manually. They can triage incidents in real time to do remediation for their enterprises.

An effective SOAR system can be a valuable tool to alleviate the strain on IT and security teams by incorporating automated responses to various events. Security teams can customize a SOAR system to fit their organization's needs.

Extended Detection and Response (XDR)

An emerging trend in detection and incident response is extended detection and response (XDR). An XDR solution collects and then correlates data across security layers, including endpoints, email, servers, cloud workloads, and the network itself. It's an alternative approach to traditional detection and incident response procedures. XDR solutions integrate detection and response across multiple environments and provide a more holistic view of threats.

In many instances, well-crafted threats are hard to detect because they hide between security silos. Incidents spread faster and fly under the radar of the SOC—ultimately causing more damage.

An XDR solution isolates and dissects these threats. It correlates each threat with individual security layers. As organizations look to reduce complexity in their environments, an effective XDR solution is able to collect, normalize, and correlate data from a wider range of sources. It allows security teams to be faster and more effective at threat detection and response.

Adaptive Cloud Security

As organizations adopt multi-cloud strategies and remote workforce policies, networks have grown more distributed and workers more dependent on cloud applications and environments. Organizations often have business-critical data and services scattered across clouds and data centers. In many cases, security solutions have not kept pace with cloud-based innovations. Organizations often end up with a heterogeneous set of technologies, with disparate cloud security controls in various cloud environments.

Further complicating matters, some organizations unknowingly find themselves in what's called the shared responsibility model, which makes the cloud provider responsible for some aspects of security and the cloud user responsible for other aspects. Therefore, it is essential to understand your service level agreements with your provider so you know who is responsible for what and do not assume anything. For example, for SaaS deployments, the provider is responsible for the availability and safe access to the application. On the other hand, the customer is responsible for platform configuration, tracking of security events, and data.

As organizations look to migrate more of their on-prem services to the cloud, they still need to have visibility and control in these environments. A cloud access security broker (CASB) sits between the cloud users and the cloud applications. It adds a layer of security by monitoring activity and ensuring policy compliance.

CASBs offer insights into users, user behavior, and the data stored in major SaaS applications. They also provide data security, data loss prevention, and threat detection capabilities.

The cloud offers organizations immense business opportunities to be agile, efficient, and cost effective. But without the right security infrastructure in place, the cloud may present serious security challenges.

Many organizations adopt a multi-cloud strategy to reduce risk (as in, don't put all your eggs in one basket). Mergers and acquisitions may force a multi-cloud strategy as can adoption of certain applications or services available on only one cloud platform.

Multi-cloud increases complexity for security teams as each cloud provider has different security tools, approaches, and configuration capabilities.

To overcome these challenges, enterprises need solutions that integrate with all major cloud providers, cover the entire attack surface, and provide centralized security management.

Conclusion

End-to-end security requires a platform that offers integrated functionality and open APIs to incorporate information and capabilities from existing tools and threat intelligence. Effective use of a security platform will integrate your operations and your threat intelligence, help you manage complexity, and provide automation to achieve speed and consistency. To meet the challenges of today and tomorrow and have a chance of getting ahead of increasingly sophisticated and automated adversaries, you need broad visibility across the entire digital attack surface. With such an end-to-end security platform, it is possible to better manage risk, reduce the complexity of supporting multiple point products, and enable automated workflows to increase the speed of operations and response.

Glossary

AI/ML

Artificial intelligence/machine learning.

API

Application programming interface.

APT

Advanced persistent threat.

AWS

Amazon Web Services.

Backdoor

Method by which users are able to get around normal security measures and gain high-level access to a system.

CapEx

Capital expenditures. Cloud adoption often moves capital expenditures (for purchasing, maintaining, and running hardware and software) to operating expenses (subscription and/or monthly usage fees).

CASB

Cloud access security broker.

CERT

Computer emergency response team.

CFO

Chief financial officer.

CGO

Chief governance officer.

CIO

Chief information officer.

CISO

Chief information security officer.

CISSP

Certified Information Systems Security Professional; a certification offered by the International Information System Security Certification Consortium (ISC)^2.

CPRA

California Privacy Rights Act.

CRO

Chief risk officer.

CSA

Cloud Security Alliance.

C-SCRM

Cyber supply chain risk management (see Chapter 10).

CCPA

California Consumer Privacy Act.

CSP

Cloud service provider.

CSPM

Cloud security posture management.

C-suite

Refers to the executive-level managers within a company. Common C-suite executives include chief executive officer (CEO), chief financial officer (CFO), chief operating officer (COO), and chief information officer (CIO).

CWPP

Cloud workload protection platform.

Dark web

Pages on the web that aren't indexed by any search engines and aren't viewable in a standard browser.

DARPA

Defense Advanced Research Projects Agency. The agency that created the ARPAnet, predecessor of the internet.

DDoS

Distributed denial of service.

DevOps

A practice in which development teams work closely with operations teams.

DHS

Department of Homeland Security.

Digital transformation

Using digital technologies to transform business processes, user experiences, and products.

DLP

Data loss protection.

DoD/IC

Department of Defense/Intelligence Community.

Doxing

The practice of publicly revealing private information about someone, such as their phone number or address.

EDR

Endpoint detection and response.

Effovation

A term coined by Susan Koski to describe a blend of efficiency and innovation (see Chapter 3).

Endpoint security

The practice of securing end-user devices such as desktops, laptops, and mobile devices from being exploited by malicious actors and campaigns.

EPP

Endpoint protection platform.

FCI

Federal contract information.

GRC

Governance, risk, and compliance.

Hacktivist

Attackers who have a political or social agenda.

Hairpinning

Traffic that enters and exits the same interface.

HR

Human resources.

IaaS

Infrastructure as a service.

IGC

Information Governance Council.

Internet of Things

The interconnection of physical objects with sensors that send and receive data.

IOC

Indicator of compromise; a forensic term that refers to the evidence on a device that points to a security breach.

IP

Internet Protocol.

ISAC

Information Sharing and Analysis Center.

ISAO

Information Sharing and Analysis Organization.

ISO

An independent, non-governmental international organization with a membership of 165 national standards bodies.

IT/OT

Information technology/operational technology.

ITaaS

IT as a service; a technology-delivery method that treats information technology as a commodity, providing an enterprise with the amount of hardware, software, and support that it needs for an agreed-on monthly fee.

KPI

Key performance indicator.

KRI

Key risk indicator.

Legacy
Older computers or software still in use.

Machine learning
A technique that allows computer systems to learn by using algorithms and statistical models to analyze and draw inferences from patterns in data.

Malware
Software designed to interfere with the normal function of a computer.

MCP
Metric control plan.

ML
Machine learning.

MPLS
Multi Protocol Label Switching.

MTA
Message transfer agent.

NAC
Network access control.

Net promoter score
An index ranging from -100 to 100 that measures the willingness of customers to recommend a company's products or services to others.

Network sniffer
Software that examines data crossing a network in real time.

NIST
National Institute of Standards and Technology.

NOC
Network Operations Center.

NSA

National Security Agency.

OKR

Objectives and key results.

OpEx

Operating expenses. Cloud adoption often moves capital expenditures (buy, house, and run the hardware) to operating expenses (subscription and/or monthly usage fees).

OWASP

Open Web Application Security Project. See Chapter 8.

PaaS

Platform as a service.

PCI-DSS

Payment Card Industry Data Security Standard.

Pen-test

Penetration testing; a simulated cyberattack performed to uncover weaknesses in an organization's security.

Phishing

The fraudulent practice of sending links purporting to be from reputable companies to induce individuals to reveal personal information or download malware.

PII

Personally identifiable information.

Ransomware

A type of malware that requires the victim to pay a ransom in order to access files the attacker has encrypted.

Risk appetite

The amount and type of risk that an organization is prepared to pursue, retain, or take.

SaaS

Software as a service; a software distribution model in which a third-party provider hosts applications and makes them available to customers over the internet.

SASE

Secure access service edge.

Script kiddie

A person who uses existing computer scripts or code to hack into computers, lacking the expertise to write their own.

SD-WAN

Software-defined wide area network.

SEG

Secure email gateway.

Shared responsibility model

A framework that divides responsibilities between a cloud service provider and the organization or individual that uses the services of that provider.

SIEM

Security information and event management.

SLA

Service-level agreement.

SOAR

Secure orchestration automation and response.

SOC

Security operations center.

SSO

Single sign-on.

STEM

A curriculum based on the idea of educating students in four specific disciplines—science, technology, engineering, and mathematics—in an interdisciplinary and applied approach.

SWG

Secure web gateway.

SWOT

Strengths, weaknesses, opportunities, and threats. A SWOT analysis is a technique for assessing these four aspects of a given problem or situation.

Threat actors

A person or entity responsible for an event or incident that impacts, or has the potential to impact, the safety or security of another entity.

TLS

Transport Layer Security.

TTP

Tactics, techniques, and procedures. The patterns that an attacker uses that can be used in threat hunting.

Unknown unknowns

Unexpected or unforeseeable conditions that pose a potentially greater risk simply because they cannot be anticipated based on past experience or investigation. Known unknowns result from recognized but poorly understood phenomena.

VLAN

Virtual local area network.

VPN

Virtual private network.

WFH

Work from home.

XDR

Extended detection and response.

XSS

Cross-site scripting, a common attack on web applications.

Zero trust

A security concept that requires all users, even insiders, to be authenticated and authorized before being granted access.

ZTA

Zero trust access.

Resources We Rely On

Relevant Sites for CISOs

(ISC)², https://www.isc2.org/

CISA (Cyber & Infrastructure Security Agency), https://www.cisa.gov/

CyberEdBoard, members-only community for security leaders, https://ismg.io/brands/cyberedboard/

Cybersecurity Collaborative, which offers resources for CISOs, https://www.cyberleadersunite.com/memberships/for-cisos

FBI, https://www.fbi.gov/

Global Cyber Alliance, https://www.globalcyberalliance.org/

IEEE, https://www.ieee.org/

InfraGard, https://www.infragard.org

National Security Institute at George Mason University, https://nationalsecurity.gmu.edu/

NSA, https://www.nsa.gov/what-we-do/cybersecurity/

SANS, https://www.sans.org/

US Chamber of Commerce, https://www.uschamber.com/national-and-cyber-security

Stay Informed of the Latest Threats

Blogs and Periodicals

Bleeping Computer, https://www.bleepingcomputer.com/

CIO, https://www.cio.com/

CRN, http://crn.com

CSO, https://www.csoonline.com/

Cybercrime Magazine, https://cybersecurityventures.com/

Dark Reading, https://www.darkreading.com/

HackerNews, https://news.ycombinator.com/

Krebs on Security Blog, https://krebsonsecurity.com/

Motherboard, https://www.vice.com/en/section/tech

Network World, https://www.networkworld.com/

Schneier on Security, https://www.schneier.com/

Security Week, https://www.securityweek.com/

ZDNet, https://www.zdnet.com/topic/security/

Follow on Twitter

Marcus J. Carey, https://twitter.com/marcusjcarey

Cyberleaders, https://twitter.com/cyberleaders

FBI, https://twitter.com/FBI

Katie Moussouris, https://twitter.com/k8em0

NSA, https://twitter.com/NSAGov

Runa Sandvik, https://twitter.com/runasand

SANS, https://twitter.com/SANSInstitute

Dino Dai Zovi, https://twitter.com/dinodaizovi

Podcasts

Daily Stormcast, https://isc.sans.edu/podcast.html

Hacker Valley Studios, https://hackervalleystudio.podbean.com/

Risky.biz, https://risky.biz/

Security Conversations, https://securityconversations.fireside.fm/

Microsoft's Security Unlocked podcast, https://securityunlockedpodcast.com/

Books

George Finney, *Well Aware: Master The Nine Cybersecurity Habits To Protect Your Future*, https://wellawaresecurity.com/bookstore-2/

Brian Krebs, *Spam Nation: The Inside Story of Organized Cybercrime-From Global Epidemic to Your Front Door*, https://bookshop.org/books/spam-nation-the-inside-story-of-organized-cybercrime-from-global-epidemic-to-your-front-door/9781492603238

Kevin Mitnick, *The Art of Deception: Controlling the Human Element of Security*, https://www.mitnicksecurity.com/the-art-of-deception

Bruce Schneier, *Click Here to Kill Everybody: Security and Survival in a Hyper-connected World*, https://www.schneier.com/books/click-here/

Adam Shostack, *Threat Modeling: Designing for Security*, https://shostack.org/books/threat-modeling-book

List of cyber-related books

Cybersecurity Canon, curated list of books from Ohio State's Institute for Cybersecurity and Digital Trust, https://icdt.osu.edu/cybercanon

Communicate Effectively with the Business

Books

Joel Garfinkle, *Getting Ahead*, https://garfinkleexecutivecoaching.com/books/getting-ahead

Dan Heath, *Upstream: The Quest to Solve Problems Before They Happen*, https://heathbrothers.com/books/upstream/

Douglas Hubbard and Richard Seiersend, *How to Measure Anything in Cybersecurity Risk*, https://www.howtomeasureanything.com/cybersecurity/

Jerry Z. Muller, *The Tyranny of Metrics*, https://press.princeton.edu/books/hardcover/9780691174952/the-tyranny-of-metrics

Alexander Osterwalder and Yves Pigneur, *Business Model Generation: A Handbook for Visionaries, Game Changers, and Challengers*, https://bookshop.org/books/business-model-generation-a-handbook-for-visionaries-game-changers-and-challengers/9780470876411

Kerry Patterson, Joseph Grenny, Ron McMillan, and Al Switzler, *Crucial Conversations: Tools for Talking When Stakes Are High*, https://bookshop.org/books/crucial-conversations-tools-for-talking-when-stakes-are-high-second-edition-9780071771320/9780071771320

Jack J. Phillips and Lynn Schmidt, *The Leadership Scorecard*, https://www.routledge.com/The-Leadership-Scorecard/Phillips-Schmidt/p/book/9780750677646

Online Resources

BoardTalk blog, https://blog.nacdonline.org/

Cyber Risk Oversight Handbook, https://isalliance.org/isa-publications/cyber-risk-oversight-handbook/

Share Data from Annual Breach and Threat Reports

Accenture, https://www.accenture.com/us-en/insights/security/cyber-threatscape-report

Crowdstrike, https://www.crowdstrike.com/resources/reports/global-threat-report/

FireEye, https://www.fireeye.com/current-threats/annual-threat-report.html

OWASP Top Ten, https://owasp.org/www-project-top-ten/

Verizon Data Breach Investigations Report, https://www.verizon.com/business/resources/reports/dbir/

World Economic Forum Global Risks Report, https://www.weforum.org/reports/the-global-risks-report-2021

Risk and Compliance

CMMC (Cybersecurity Maturity Model Certification), https://www.acq.osd.mil/cmmc/

How to Make Sense of Cybersecurity Frameworks by Frank Kim, SANS, https://youtu.be/dt2IqidgpS4

Cyber Supply Chain Risk Management (C-SCRM) References, https://csrc.nist.gov/scrm/references.html

ISO 28000, https://www.iso.org/standard/44641.html

ISO 20243, https://www.iso.org/standard/74399.html

ISO 31000 risk management standard, https://www.iso.org/iso-31000-risk-management.html

MITRE ATT&CK framework knowledge base, https://attack.mitre.org/

NIST Cybersecurity Framework, https://www.nist.gov/cyberframework

NIST SP 800-171, https://csrc.nist.gov/publications/detail/sp/800-171/rev-2/final

Conferences to Attend

RSA Conference, https://www.rsaconference.com/

Gartner cybersecurity conferences, https://www.gartner.com/en/conferences/calendar/security-risk-management

FIRST Incident Response Conference https://www.first.org/conference/

Many events

Infosec-Conferences.com, Cybersecurity conference and event aggregator, https://infosec-conferences.com/

Increase Diversity and Inclusion

Diversity

International Consortium of Minority Cybersecurity Professionals, https://www.icmcp.org/

Diversity Wins: How Inclusion Matters, https://www.mckinsey.com/featured-insights/diversity-and-inclusion/diversity-wins-how-inclusion-matters

Women

Executive Women's Forum, https://www.ewf-usa.com/

Risky Women, https://riskywomen.org/

WiCyS - Women in Cybersecurity, https://www.wicys.org/

Women of Security (WoSEC), https://www.womenofsecurity.com/

Women's Society of Cyberjutsu, https://womenscyberjutsu.org/

Society of Women Engineers, https://swe.org/

Training and Certifications

(ISC)² offers major certifications including CISSP, SSCP, CCSP, CAP, CSSLP or HCISPP, https://www.isc2.org/

National Initiative for Cybersecurity Careers and Studies, https://niccs.cisa.gov/training

ICE - National Initiative for Cybersecurity Education, https://www.nist.gov/itl/applied-cybersecurity/nice

Open Security Training, https://www.opensecuritytraining.info/Training.html

Georgia Tech network security course, https://www.udacity.com/course/network-security--ud199

Promote Security Awareness

National Cybersecurity Alliance, with free tools and information to support employee security awareness programs, https://staysafeonline.org/

National Cybersecurity Awareness Month, https://www.cisa.gov/national-cyber-security-awareness-month

Cloud Security

Cloud Security Alliance, https://cloudsecurityalliance.org/

Secure Development

CMU Software Engineering Institute Cybersecurity Engineering, https://www.sei.cmu.edu/our-work/cybersecurity-engineering/

OWASP (Open Web Application Security Project), https://owasp.org/

Tools

Burp Suite, https://portswigger.net/burp

ZAP (Zed Attack Proxy), https://www.zaproxy.org/

Hacker Conferences

Bsides, http://securitybsides.com

Shmoocon, https://www.shmoocon.org/

GrrCon, https://grrcon.com/

SummerCon, https://www.summercon.org/

DefCon, http://defcon.org

Black Hat, https://www.blackhat.com/

IoT Security

IoT Security 101, https://github.com/V33RU/IoTSecurity101#Books-For-IoT-Pentesting

Industrial Control Systems Security, https://www.sans.org/industrial-control-systems-security/

Industry-Specific Resources

ISAC (Information Sharing and Analysis Centers) for many industries, https://www.nationalisacs.org/member-isacs-3

Financial Services Information Sharing and Analysis Center, https://www.fsisac.com/

Healthcare

Association for Executives in Healthcare Information Security, https://aehis.org/

CHIME (College of Healthcare Information Management Executives), https://chimecentral.org/

HIMSS (Healthcare Information and Management Systems Society), https://www.himss.org/

Massachusetts Health Data Consortium, https://www.mahealthdata.org/page-1861560

Fill the Future Skills Pipeline

FBI Cybercamp, https://www.infragardnational.org/programs/cyber-camp-in-a-box/

NICE - National Initiative for Cybersecurity Education, https://www.nist.gov/itl/applied-cybersecurity/nice

Girls Who Code, https://girlswhocode.com/

Cyber Talent Initiative, get a job that comes with $75K in student loan assistance, https://cybertalentinitiative.org/

CyberStart America, program for high school students, https://www.cyberstartamerica.org/

Index

identifying and tagging of, 187
open risk data, 149
possibility for degradation,
  contamination, and vulnerabilities
  of, 174
protection of, 187
sharing of, 83, 218
unstructured data dilemma, 173
data breach, average cost of, 194. *See also*
  specific breaches
Data Governance Council, 79
data loss protection (DLP), 174
decision-making, 119, 121
Department of Homeland Security
  (DHS), warnings from about
  cyberattacks, 46
device-specific approach, risks of, 172
DevOps, 103
DevSecOps, 103
distributed denial-of-service (DDoS)
  attacks, 45
diversity
  power of, 61–62
  resources for increasing, 219–220
diversity gap, 7–8, 60–64
Docker Hub breach, 162
Dropbox, 183
due diligence, 176
dynamic application security testing
  (DAST), 106, 107

E

edge devices, 170–174, 176
edge points, 169, 171, 175, 176
edge security, 157–158, 169
effectiveness, measurement of, as cultural
  element of security, 30
8-K SEC form, 108
encryption, 129, 186, 187, 197
endpoint detection and response (EDR),
  201
endpoint protection, 200
endpoint protection platform (EPP), 201
endpoint security, 200, 201
end-to-end security, 158–159, 193–204
engagement, measuring of, as cultural
  element of security, 30

Enterprise Risk Management (ERM)
  Committee, 78–79, 82
executive leadership, CISOs' need to work
  with, 96
extended detection and response (XDR),
  200, 202–203
external threats, 44–47

F

Facebook breach, 162
FAIR, risk framework 127
false positives, 98, 106, 107
FAR 52.204-21, 146
FDA, pacemaker recall over concerns that
  devices could be compromised, 171
Federal Information Processing
  Standards (FIPS) publication 200,
  146
Florida, unauthorized user attempting
  to change formula of public water
  supply in, 171
Forbes Technology Council, on benefits
  of closing cybersecurity's gender
  gap, 61
frameworks, 127, 128–130, 141–143.
  See also ISO framework; NIST
  Cybersecurity Framework

G

Gartner, on SASE, 197
GCP (Google Cloud Platform),
  161, 182
gender gap, in cybersecurity,
  60, 61
glossary, 205–214
Gmail, 183, 186
GoDaddy breach, 162
Google, on encryption of traffic in transit,
  193
Google Drive, 182
governance
  changing role of, 117–131
  problem of poor cyber governance,
  162
governance, risk, and compliance
  (GRC), 117-131